# Parallel Lives

## A Novel Way to Learn
## Thinking and Writing

James M. Wallace
*King's College*
*Wilkes Barre, Pennsylvania*

The McGraw-Hill Companies, Inc.
Primis Custom Publishing

New York   St. Louis   San Francisco   Auckland   Bogotá
Caracas   Lisbon   London   Madrid   Mexico   Milan   Montreal
New Delhi   Paris   San Juan   Singapore   Sydney   Tokyo   Toronto

**McGraw·Hill**

A Division of The **McGraw·Hill** Companies

Parallel Lives
A Novel Way to Learn Thinking and Writing

McGraw-Hill's Primis Custom Publishing consists of products that are produced from camera-ready copy. Peer review, class testing, and accuracy are primarily the responsibility of the author(s).

1 2 3 4 5 6 7 8 9 0 GDP GDP 9 0 9 8 7

ISBN 07-012260-1

Editor: Constance Ditzel
Printer/Binder: Greyden Press

# Foreword

Associate professor of English at King's College, Wilkes-Barre, Pennsylvania, James M. Wallace has devised a book that should delight the reader in its accurate portrayal of college life, but that also invites students and teachers of critical thinking and writing to join the fictional Professor Watkins and his students on their journey through the study of these two disciplines.

The outbreak of a racial incident on a small college campus becomes the occasion of a classroom workshop in critical thinking as students are given the tools to make sound judgments about the disturbing events. The orchestrator of this learning process is a young assistant professor, Peter Watkins, a gentle and sensitive man who inspires his students to learn about themselves through writing, encouraging them to "look within" and answer the age-old question, "Who am I?" and through critical thinking to examine their world intelligently and insightfully. Watkins insists that college must not be a hollow, ivory tower experience, but rather that it must provide, both in and out of class, learning that is applicable to their everyday lives. Paralleling his touching the hearts and minds of his students, profoundly affecting the growth of two particular students, Watkins is also taught by them as he discovers that, contrary to the principal tenets of his teaching philosophy, he has in his personal life not "taken risks" and "become involved."

The author has created a new genre—a novel combined with a textbook or primer for two disciplines. Reflecting his personal experience, the novel deals realistically with college life. Those who really know what college life is all about will admire the truth portrayed—how seldom do authors ever get it right! Additionally, from his own extensive and serious endeavors in these two disciplines, Jim Wallace has provided for faculty, many of whom have despaired of ever finding suitable textbooks and approaches to critical thinking and writing, a book they may find most promising and effective. To make the book even more accessible to both students and teachers, a sizable lesson guide is provided.

His colleagues and students will readily see truth meeting fiction in this portrayal of a highly effective teacher sensitive to the needs of his students and committed to their education. As colleague and friend, I am honored that Jim has trusted me to help edit this innovative enterprise.

Louis Rader
Professor of English

*To the reader:*

Although I hope that the characters in *Parallel Lives* seem authentic, they are not real. I made them up. Yes, I took many of the descriptions and traits, the attitudes and dialogue from the thousands of students I've taught in the past seventeen years, but no one single student served as the model for any character in the book. The same is true of the several professors in the novel. No correlation will be discovered between the professionals in the book and my colleagues present or past. Mom, Dad, sisters of mine: any positive portrayal of family members was inspired by you; any negative portrayal should be seen as an accurate depiction of our cousins.

*Parallel Lives* differs from other textbooks in that it is a fictional work. I do not pretend in this novel that the professor depicted is teaching thinking and writing in the only way it can be or ought to be taught. The professor and the students in the novel present opinions and conclusions that I hope the reader will consider, but that ultimately can be accepted, rejected or modified. The extensive list of questions at the end of the book invites students to think about the various questions and issues that arise in the novel. Students should understand that their own professors may disagree with the conclusions drawn by the professor in the book.

I owe a great debt to a great many people, especially my colleagues in the English and Philosophy Departments at King's College, the secretarial pool of Hafey-Marian Hall (Betty Didgeon, Anita Grigor, Sandy Kase, and Donna Kazmierski), Constance Ditzel and Annie Williams at McGraw-Hill, my family and friends. The debt I owe my wife, Deborah Ann, can never be paid (she has said so); she patiently endured my constant revising and read every word of every draft. For her suggestions and improvements, I thank her. For her patience, humor and tenderness, I revere her.

Finally, I could not have accomplished this book without the help of my colleague and friend, Dr. Louis Rader. The forty-page *Learning Guide* that follows the text, which he wrote almost single-handedly, is his least significant contribution to the project. He is a keen editor, a sensitive reader, and among the most generous men I have ever met. I am happy to pay him the highest compliment I know of: he has been my greatest teacher.

JMW

*For Debbie*

# CHAPTER I

# Tuesday, August 26

## John Zajaczkiewicz

John Zajaczkiewicz was an exceptionally handsome young man, but you'd never know it by looking at him. All his life he had been awfully self-conscious, and to make the point certain, he wore a salt-stained Seattle Mariners baseball cap with the bill curving almost in a perfect half-circle and hanging like a window awning over his eyes. If someone addressed him, he bent his head forward just enough to shadow his face and shield himself from the glare of his tormentor. Throughout high school, the cap had been something of a trademark, but not in the way the more popular kids were known by their various body piercings, tattoos, footwear, cigarette brand or how late into the evening they wore their sunglasses. This hat had become his identity. Because he played no sports, belonged to no clubs, attended no homecomings, pep rallies, dances or proms, avoided yearbook photographers, kept silent in class, and walked home the moment the school day ended, few of his classmates even knew his name, and most referred to him simply as "that kid in the Mariners cap." He was in the true sense of the word a "loner," a curiosity among the other students and the source of constant speculation.

When John walked into Room 312 at ten minutes before nine on his first day of college, he walked as if he had been programmed, past the professor and straight to the back of the room, where he took the last seat in the left-hand corner. Years of classroom study had taught him that most teachers tended to look primarily toward the right side of the room during lectures and that his chances of remaining happily anonymous for fifteen weeks were best if he sat in the back left. As he walked toward his seat, he surmised from the professor's Nikes and Levis that he was a fairly young man, and in his peripheral vision John could see one other student in the room—in the dead center of the room, in fact. *How could she do that,* he thought, *with an empty room to choose from?*

Waiting for class to begin, John doodled a large "S" and compass points on the cover of his notebook and thought about the night before. Deliberately arriving late to avoid Orientation "ice breaker" games and

3

group discussions, he found his dorm room with the help of his mother and settled in with the few boxes of clothes and supplies they had jammed into her ten-year-old Tercel.

"I'm sorry I couldn't get you a car, John," she'd told him as if saying it for the first time. "You could have drove the eighty miles every day if I could have got you a car."

John assured her that he didn't regret his choice. "I'll be fine here. I can get the bus if things get too hard for me. Besides, this place might help me, you know, get along better—a baptism of fire, as they say."

They said their good-byes in tears, his mother making no effort to conceal hers and John worrying that at any moment his roommate could walk in on the spectacle. As he walked her down the stairs and to her car, she made him swear to call everyday, at least for the first few weeks, and promised to come for him if he wanted to go home on weekends. He watched her drive away and knew that hearing her voice on the phone wasn't going to be enough; he was going to miss the one person whose face he could look into without panic or terror, the one person with whom he could honestly express his deepest feelings.

From the back of the room, John could hear the shuffle of feet, the screech of chair legs on linoleum, the unzipping of knapsacks. He caught a few subdued conversations, but mostly he could hear only the quiet settling in of students on the first day of class. Suddenly, like an alarm clock going off on the morning of his adult life, he heard the first words of a college professor: "Hello, everyone. My name is Peter Watkins, and I know I'm not the first person to welcome you to Wexford College, but let me add my warmest greetings."

*Actually,* John thought, *You are the first to welcome me, thank you.* As Watkins read the roster, John sat listening to the array of names: Albright. *I wonder if she is.* Churnip. *I'll bet he had a hard time with that name.* Theodore somebody. A couple of Jennifers. A Jessica something that Watkins pronounced variously as "Wang" "Who-ang" and "How-wong" (fortunately, the student preferred "Jessica"). One guy with two first names. Only one person not present, an Eileen something. And a girl with an awfully embarrassing name, he thought. He wondered why her father didn't have it changed. *Does he give that name when he's waiting for a table at a restaurant?* Then he sat up. *Here it comes,* he thought. *Thirteen years of school and every new class.*

"John Zaaajjj . . ., Za-jack . . ., Zaaaaaaaa."

"Zah-yonch-KEH-veech," John said quietly, almost inaudibly.

"Zah-yonch-KEH-veech, John Zah-yonch-KEH-veech," Watkins repeated.

"Yes."

"Do you have any nicknames, John?"

*Do I!?* John thought, *"Z," "Z-jack," "Z-boy," "Zines-ketchup," and a thousand other childish, nonsense words beginning with Z.* "No," he said, "just John."

"I'll bet you've been the last student listed on every roster since you started school."

*Great*, thought John. *Draw attention to it.* "Yeah," he said, trying to halt Watkins's apparent fascination as quickly as possible.

"You have one of those names that, if it were the name of a character in a novel, readers would just skip over it. Are you from around here, John? I'm guessing your name is Polish. Names like yours aren't that uncommon in this area."

John's thoughts raced: *Jesus Christ! What's he doing? Why's he abusing me? No one else got this stupid inquisition.* He could hear the other students twisting in their seats as they turned to look at Zaaajjj-- something. "I'm from Devon," he said.

"Oh, a few hours west of here," Watkins said. "That's a pretty part of the State. I thought maybe you were from Seattle."

John just shook his head lightly but rapidly and felt the blood rushing from his face as Watkins went on to distribute and discuss the syllabus. Skimming the paper quickly to see if there were any oral reports scheduled, John relaxed when he saw only essays. Essays he could handle. Tests? No problem. Oral reports? He had pleaded with his mother to call the high school principal and tell her that his uncle had been killed in a car accident and that the funeral was on the same day as graduation so that—God, they were just sick over the whole thing— John's salutatory speech would have to be delivered by someone else. His mother wouldn't budge.

In the class, everyone else also seemed to be speed reading the syllabus to determine how much work the course entailed.

"Six papers! This dude's nuts," John heard.

He looked to his left at another baseball-capped student waiting for commiseration on the excessive amount of work Watkins required. John just shrugged and returned his attention to Watkins. Much of what the professor said was interesting, and some comments were genuinely funny, but John knew that his fellow first-year students were not comfortable enough to laugh, that they didn't yet know if it was okay to laugh. And as a student, John knew the dangers of appearing too eager, too interested or too entertained. You could end up wearing some embarrassing label for an entire semester. Watkins wasn't taking too many risks with the comedy, John thought. Things were going well. He was sure Watkins was going to be a fair and decent teacher, and looking around the room, he could sense that most of his class-mates agreed. John noticed that Watkins faltered here and there in his reading of the syllabus, lost his place one or twice, but overall things moved along smoothly.

The sudden noise of a door opening caught John's attention, and he looked up. Slowly into the room came without a doubt the most beauti-ful girl he had ever seen—darkly tanned and tall, dressed in a white tee-shirt and a short denim skirt, no makeup, no jewelry, no bag, no pen or pencil, no books, nothing but an aura of confidence and wealth. She said something to Watkins, took a syllabus and quickly scanned the room for an empty seat. Although there were several, including some in the first row, she set her sights on one clear across the room and in the back. *Of course,* thought John, *choosing a seat in the front row wouldn't have allowed her to walk the runway.* As she glided among his dazed, staring classmates, John created for her an entire life of front lawns and circular driveways, of catered graduation parties under tents, of Toyota 4-Runners and ski vacations. Not only was she late for the first day of class, but she was late *and* rich *and* beautiful. You had to hate her.

### Peter Watkins

On his first official day as an assistant professor, exactly three and a half months after receiving his Ph.D. and two days after his twenty-eighth birthday, Professor Peter Watkins stood looking at the syllabus he would in a few moments distribute to his class of first-year writers. He'd stood in front of freshman classes as a graduate teaching fellow, but he'd always considered himself just a slightly older version of the students he attempted to teach, as if he'd been asked by the real teacher to keep an eye on things until she returned. And besides, he never really believed that he would actually finish graduate school and find a job. He knew far more almost-finished Ph.D.'s than finished ones and several housepainters with Ph.D.'s who were "never all that interested in teaching anyway." But here he was.

As he looked at the syllabus, he was convinced that it contained typographical errors somewhere and that his students would lose all respect for him as a writing teacher as soon as they discovered them. He knew, too, that if he found the errors before he handed out the syllabus, he could point them out nonchalantly, as if he had known about them for years but had been too busy or unconcerned to correct them. It occurred to him, as it always did, that he could offhandedly blame "the secretary," an imaginary person since he had typed the syllabus himself. As he read, his students began filing into the room. He scanned more quickly: "six papers of 750 words each," "attendance is mandatory," "late papers will not be accepted," "text . . . ," "office hours . . . ," and so on. Nothing was amiss, but he kept reading, trying to give the appearance of doing something important so that he could avoid making eye contact with the twenty students who had trickled through the door for the past ten minutes and who now sat almost silently waiting for him to begin class. Could they possibly know that their professor, who had survived a hundred seminar reports in front of the most competitive and combative fellow graduate students, who had defended his research to the most renowned scholars in the country, who had practiced his teaching methods for seven years, had knots in his stomach the size of baseballs and that he was still unsure of what mask to wear on the first day—that of the stern taskmaster who failed late papers, or that of the person he really was, the gentle, infinitely patient, and somewhat timid young man who very seldom met his own deadlines and avoided suffering the pangs of hypocrisy by never having failed even the latest papers?

At precisely 9:00—he had at the last moment selected the taskmaster persona and wanted to give the impression that he did not tolerate lateness—Watkins spoke.

"Hello, everyone. My name is Peter Watkins, and I know I'm not the first person to welcome you to Wexford College, but let me add my warmest greetings. The first thing I'm going to do this morning is take roll to make sure that you're all in the right room. Please forgive me if I butcher your name and let me know the correct pronunciation. And let me know if you like to be called by a nickname. He looked at the first name, an easy one: "Ann Marie Albright."

"Here."

"Is that what you like to be called? 'Ann Marie'?"

"Yes."

Watkins underlined the entire first name on his roster.

Another easy one: "Theodore Crossings."

"Here."

"Do you go by a shorter form? 'Ted'? 'Teddy'?"

"No. Theodore."

*That's right,* Watkins remembered to himself, *there are no more Teds, or Petes, or Johns, or Chrises, or Bettys. Now everyone is Theodore or Peter or Jonathan or Christian or Elizabeth or the occasional Whatever.* He decided not to ask.

"Peter Churnip."

"Here. Pete."

"Pardon?" asked Watkins, thinking he had been casually addressed.

"Call me 'Pete.'"

"You like to be called 'Pete'?"

"Yeah."

He made it through the list without too many embarrassments. "Hjelm" had tripped him up. *Oh, yeah, silent "j."* After enduring three attempts to accurately repeat her name, a Vietnamese-American student mercifully settled for Watkins's last attempt and asked to be called Jessica. Only one absentee—an Eileen O'Neill. And Watkins deliberately mispronounced one name because the alternative pronunciation—the correct one, as it turned out—was a silly synonym for a male body part. He didn't want to take the chance of being wrong, so he figured he'd let the student pronounce it. And then he came to the last name, a killer. He knew he was going to screw this up royally: "John Zaaajjj . . ., Zajack . . ., Zaaaaaaaa."

"Zah-yonch-KEH-veech," he thought he heard.

"Zah-yonch-KEH-veech," Watkins repeated slowly, and again, carefully, John Zah-yonch-KEH-veech" trying to show that he really wanted to get this right, that he cared, and that names, like all words, were important to him. Mr. Zajaczkiewicz looked insulted by the bungled pronunciation of his name, so, figuring he'd relax him with a little friendly chatter, Watkins referred to the cap John wore. Watkins had learned long ago that a student's baseball cap was often his most distinguishing characteristic, better than a mustache, eyeglasses, earring, acne, a wild haircut, big ears or a handsome face. One time in graduate school at the end of a semester, a young man who was not wearing a baseball cap came up to him on campus and asked about the final paper. "Do I know you?" Watkins asked him. It turned out to be someone who sat in the front row of Watkins's afternoon composition class. Seeing a student without his cap has the effect of seeing a man who has shaved himself bald. But in this case, knowing that the "S" on Zahyonch-KEH-veech's cap indicated the Seattle Mariners earned Watkins no points. The student seemed to resent Watkins's attention. He felt the blood rushing into his face and moved on.

As Watkins distributed the syllabus he told the class what he had planned for the next fifteen weeks. For Watkins this was always the hardest part—much more difficult than clumsy introductory moments of the first class or the bungled calling of the role. Did it look like too much work? Would they hate him even before they got to know him, before he had a chance to teach them anything? Why didn't they find this comment funny or that one interesting? *This isn't going well*, he convinced himself. The syllabus was suddenly swimming with typos—words misspelled, words missing, words typed upside down. Watkins stammered along until the door suddenly opened and in walked a young woman who looked a lot like a hundred other young women who had walked into and through Watkins's classroom and his life.

"Is this Room 312?" she asked very quietly.

*Unless the big 3-1-2-on the door is a practical joke,* Watkins said to himself. "Yes, it is," he said to the young woman. "You must be Eileen."

"I'm sorry," he heard her say very, very quietly.

Watkins handed her a syllabus, and, as she walked to her seat, he tried to find his place in the squirming mass of small black lines on the page in front of him.


### Eileen O'Neill

Eileen O'Neill parked her beat-up Chevy Cavalier in the first spot she saw, even though she was three blocks from campus, and half-walked, half-ran to the Humanities Building. Standing outside the door of Room 312, she felt her heart beat so loudly that she was certain everyone in the room was wondering about the noise. She took a few deep breaths and turned the doorknob. She'd forgotten to prepare a comment for the professor, and so she said the first thing that came to mind—"Is this Room 312?"— realizing a moment too late that it sounded pretty dumb. She could feel the gaze of everyone on her, so, avoiding eye contact, she quickly glanced over the room and choose the first open seat that her sight locked onto. When she sat down, she noticed the other dozen or so empty seats, most of them in the front row, some of them near the door. She could have avoided the humiliating waltz across the room had she been less nervous and more observant. Well, she'd made her entrance. This was going to be one long semester.

She looked at the front of the syllabus to make sure that she was in the right class—English 100: Writing for College, Section B, Tuesdays and Thursdays at 9:00, Professor Watkins. Right class, but nine a.m. was not going to be easy, she realized. Her grandmother and sister were seldom fully awake before 8:00, which left precious little time for breakfast and some of the other tasks she liked to complete before she left the house in the morning—small things like gathering her books and finding a pen.

She tried to clear her mind and concentrate on Watkins's announcements. *When am I going to have time for all this?* she thought. Beginning to feel a wave of panic, she stopped listening to Watkins, certain that she'd have neither the time nor the desire to fulfill the requirements in such a demanding class. She started thinking about her lost summer spent pulling weeds in a minimum wage city job, about her friends and her father, about her mother and about her loneliness. She passed the entire period fading in and out of attention until she heard Watkins dismiss the class and remind them that their first assignment was due in the following class. She hung back and watched the other students place their syllabus between the pages of their book, or carefully place it in fresh binders or folders, or jam it into a book bag, and waited until everyone had left the room before approaching Watkins with the syllabus held out in front of her.

"I'm sorry," she said. "I won't be needing this. I'm dropping the class."

Watkins looked surprised and concerned. "You've decided so quickly? What's wrong?"

"I just won't have time to complete all this work," Eileen said apologetically. "I'm not a full-time student, and I just thought I'd try to take a few classes, but I didn't realize how much work there'd be." She thought for a moment that Watkins might think he'd done something to scare her away. "It's not you," she said. "I just don't think I could handle it."

"It always seems a bit intimidating on the first day," Watkins assured her. "Why don't you give it a few weeks? Try the first assignment and see how you do. If you decide that"—he paused momentarily—"you're not interested, you can always drop then."

Watkins wasn't very persuasive, but Eileen was beginning to feel uncomfortable, as if she had decided not to buy something but couldn't escape the aggressive salesclerk. "Okay," she said without conviction, "I'll do the first assignment." She had no intention of doing anything of the sort, but out of curiosity she looked at the instructions for the assignment as she walked out the room and down the steps:

> **Writing Exercise.** In approximately 200 words,
> answer the following question: "Who are you?"

Eileen laughed out loud.

Reaching her car, she snapped the parking ticket from under the windshield wiper, waved it in front of her and thought, *One more reason to forget about this stupid idea.* She turned the key in the ignition and while she listened angrily to the car threatening not to start, she asked out loud, "Who am I? Who am I? I'll tell you who I am. I'm the teenage daughter of a dead mother, that's who." And despite herself, she began writing the exercise in her mind.

### *Watkins*

The late student was settled and Watkins gained his composure enough to realize that his typing was fine and that the students staring at him and at the document in front of them cared far less about his typing skills—good or bad—and much more about the excessive amount of work he had the nerve to assign. From the squirming and sighing, he could sense their displeasure, and he did everything he could think of to soft-pedal the requirements. "It looks like a lot of work, I know," he said, "but it'll get easier as you go along. Don't get nervous. I'll do everything I can to help you get through the semester and to learn how to write."

11

They weren't buying it. The kid with the unpronounceable name in the back of the room—Watkins had already forgotten even his first name—the kid in the Mariners cap, just kept looking down. The late girl stared straight ahead as if she'd been drugged. Other students slumped or shifted as if they'd been sitting for days on park benches.

Watkins thought of something to help calm them: "It's not like all six papers are due at once at the end of the semester. They're spread out over the fifteen weeks. In fact, the first writing exercise is due the next time we meet." Brilliant! The slumping students were now resting the base of their skulls against the back of their chairs. Watkins took some consolation from the handful of students who were eagerly recording the assignment in whatever special place they had designated for such notes, but he knew from experience that if he said anything more, he'd sound too apologetic and uncertain of his own purpose, or he'd have to resuscitate several of the more panicked students. Besides, they looked like they hated him enough already. "Trust me," he said and, choosing precisely the wrong topic to follow with, went on to discuss the school's policy regarding mandatory attendance.

Convinced that the number of students attending the second class would fit in his tiny office, Watkins nonetheless forged ahead. He assured the class that they all had something to say and could say it well; he talked about brainstorming for ideas, developing a thesis and outlining an essay. He told them about the writing process and about the difference between a rough draft and the final version.

After about forty minutes of the seventy-five-minute class had passed, he dismissed them: "Please read the directions for the first assignment and come to class on Thursday with the assignment completed. That's all for today."

He tried to make eye contact with the students as they shuffled out the door. He tried to assure them with a smile that he was a friendly guy and that they'd have no trouble in this course. He thought of begging them not to drop the course and making his Chair and Dean and the tenure committee wonder what the hell he was doing. He just kept smiling and nodding and looking silly. When the stream of students flowing out the door ended, Watkins turned to find the late girl coming directly toward him.

"I'm sorry," she said. "I won't be needing this. I'm dropping the class."

Watkins's desperation quickly expressed itself as ridicule: *Can't handle it, huh?* he thought to himself, but to Eileen he showed concern, and using his charm and powers of persuasion, he convinced her to stay for a week and try the first assignment. The late girl left, and Watkins went to his office to replay mentally every moment of the past forty minutes.

### John

John had heard little of what Watkins said after the rich, arrogant girl arrived late. John couldn't stop thinking about her, but he resisted the urge to look over at her more than once. Most guys that John knew fell into two categories—those that wouldn't look at a gorgeous woman (or at least would never risk getting caught) because they wouldn't want the woman to know that someone considered her worth looking at, and the other group that would stare openly and sometimes grunt or whistle or hoot as if finding just the right sound would make a woman forget her religion, morality, taste, and survival instinct and come running to his bed. In John's case it was simply mortification. He had once been spotted checking out a girl in high school and had looked away so quickly when she turned toward him that he cracked his head on the corner of an open cabinet door in the biology lab. He managed to concentrate enough through the pain and dizziness to find his way out of the classroom, down the hall and to the lavatory, where he stood bleeding into the sink. Even with no sharp objects nearby this time, he wasn't taking any chances. He stayed focused on the syllabus and examined every detail of her image in his mind.

When Watkins dismissed the class, John sneaked a quick look toward his left and eased out of the room with the other students. Because he had no other class until the afternoon, he headed straight for his dorm. He couldn't quite figure out exactly how he felt—still nervous, momentarily homesick, excited about writing, and stunned at Eileen's beauty. Marveling at the sound of her name, he suddenly felt a queasiness come over him. At first sight she had inspired something in him. Now he remembered that she was far beyond his grasp and that the presence of someone like her would only intensify his debilitating shyness. He knew that someone like her would be the source of endless misery.

Reaching his room, John sat on the bed to begin his essay. He loved to write and was eager to start. He looked over the directions:

> **Writing Exercise.** In approximately 200 words, answer the following question: "Who are you?" Remember that this is a very rough, unpolished writing exercise. I'm interested primarily in seeing what ideas you have and how you develop them. Although I will read your work, this first assignment will not be graded. You'll use this exercise to help you discover some ideas for a more formal paper. One more word of advice: 200 words is approximately one typed, double spaced page or two to three handwritten pages depending on the size of your handwriting. Don't count words; just say what you want to say.

John liked this approach—no preliminaries required, no outlines, no note cards, just stream-of-consciousness writing, the kind he enjoyed most. He plunged right in: "Call me John. Some years ago, I was born with a last name, but don't trouble yourself with that." Suddenly the door to the room flew open, slamming against the back of the desk chair. John's first thoughts were of gratitude for having chosen to work on the bed. He had no time for second thoughts.

"Where you been? I thought maybe I had a single room. Course, I wasn't here last night; my girlfriend goes here. Sophomore. I stayed at her apartment last night. Probably will any night she'll let me. So maybe you'll be the one with the single room. Ha, a Mariners fan! I can't stand them. Have you been to class? Where you from? What's your name?"

John thought while he listened that if he were writing this monologue there'd be no punctuation. What question should he answer first? Did he have to answer any? What was this guy on? "My name's John. I'm from Devon."

"I'm Nick. 'Devon'? Where's that? What time is it?"

John looked at the clock-radio, which was clearly visible to both of them. "It's ten after ten."

"Shit! Gotta go. See you later, John. Nice meetin' ya."

John cringed as Nick slammed the door behind him. He recalled filling out a questionnaire over the summer indicating his preferences in a roommate: quiet, serious student, non-smoker. He looked around the room for ashtrays.

"It was certainly not the name I would have chosen," he wrote, returning to his essay, then pausing, unable to stop thinking about Nick, how confident, even how selfish he seemed. John looked around the room, trying to get a sense of his roommate from the way Nick had "decorated" the place. If a person's major could be determined from the posters he stuck to the painted cinder block walls of his cell, Nick was a bio major, specifically anatomy, more specifically female anatomy. Three of the four posters featured inhumanely slender, colossal breasted young models, some of whom apparently owed their figures to beer-drinking. Knowing that familiarity leads to detachment, John knew that these posters, like all adornment, would eventually disappear to the eye of the person who had placed them. He knew that Nick hadn't hung these posters so much for his own enjoyment as to tell the world who he was. Who was this guy who slept at his girlfriend's apartment on the first night at school and adorned his living space with actual-size pictures of Tyra Banks? Seeking an answer, John stared at Rebecca Romijn and her Miller Lite until he forgot the question.

### *Eileen*

Eileen turned up the car radio to drown out the noise coming from the hole in her muffler. The radio was tuned to an all-talk station that her mother had often listened to and that made Eileen nostalgic. A psychologist, Dr. Sally Sprego, was ruthlessly demeaning a caller married to a man fifteen years her senior. "What was your fantasy?" demanded Sally, suggesting that the caller had secretly desired to marry her own father. Confused by the question, the caller stammered. Sally repeated the question in a clipped, smug tone that made it sound as if the question were the obvious one in this situation. Sally abused the caller unrelentingly, laughing derisively at the woman's attempts to defend her life's decisions. In self-defense, the caller finally hung up, giving Sally the opportunity to continue ridiculing her to the audience.

The next caller confessed to being a working mother, and Sally unleashed her full righteous fury. Already angered by the day's events, Eileen turned off the radio, deciding that the noise from a leaky muffler was far preferable to the shriek of a charlatan making money from the debasement of people who needed advice. She thought of the number of people who had been so kind to her grandfather and of all the others—those who were uncomfortable around illness or desensitized from its constant presence or too unimaginative to empathize with the sick. She was thinking about the changes she had noticed in herself over the past few years, when she stopped for a red light. She heard the car on her left pull up beside her before she saw it. The music was so loud that the metal in her own car was humming. Failing to resist the urge to look, she glanced at the other driver. A young man of about twenty, he was staring right at her. She turned away. When the light changed, she waited to let him get ahead of her. He wasted no time, chirping his tires as he pulled away. *Asshole*, Eileen thought.

She parked in front of her house, went inside, kissed her grandmother and asked if she needed anything. "No, I'm fine," her grandmother said. "Maybe open a window." On the television, Eileen could hear someone screaming through sobs—"You are the father. Yes, you are. Why don't you just face it? Yes, you are."—followed by wild cheering and whooping.

"Why do you watch this stuff, Nan?" Eileen asked in a voice marked more by sympathy than exasperation.

"I don't know. It distracts me. How was school?" Her grandmother's tone was so flat that Eileen could barely tell that she'd been asked a question.

"Fine, Nana. Just fine."

Eileen went into the kitchen, opened the window above the sink, and stood looking out at the backyard with tears forming in her eyes. That spot in the kitchen always brought back a flood of memories. She returned to the living room. "Nana, I have some work to do already. Do you believe it! Yell if you need anything." She kissed her grandmother on the cheek and walked up the stairs to her room. With the spiral notebook she had bought for the writing class, Eileen sat on the bed and opened to the first page. She could hear the television below. Okay, she thought, you want to know who I am? I'll tell you who I am.


### John

Catching himself in his daydream, John returned to his writing. Working fast and effortlessly, he wrote about his happy childhood

16

spent playing war and riding bicycles with his friends around the neighborhood, about his kind and loving father—a captain in the state police, about his own part-time job as stringer for the local paper, about his travels to Iceland and Australia, and about his dreams of becoming an international reporter for CNN. Even though he was writing without a pattern or purpose, John wrote by habit a well-organized and flaw-lessly structured paper, with fully developed paragraphs, neat transitions, concrete details and even a thesis sentence. By the time he finished, the essay covered five hand-written pages, greatly exceeding the two-hundred word minimum.

John closed his notebook and looked at the clock. Noon. He wasn't hungry, but he figured that he'd better eat to keep his stomach from growling in his afternoon class. He loathed going to the cafeteria and meeting new people, but nothing—not even a stupid answer—embar-rasses a student more than a rumbling stomach, he reasoned. After waiting in line to present his ID, he picked up a tray, and pondered whether he wanted "meatballs" on his spaghetti, when he heard a very loud voice in the line behind him: "Hey, John!" Startled, he reminded himself that John was a common name. "Hey, John Mariner." He didn't know anyone here. Oh, yes, he did, he remembered. He turned around and waved feebly.

"Hey, Nick."

"Looks like we're on the same schedule. Wait for me. I'll sit with ya," Nick yelled. John thought of pretending not to hear Nick—a trick that had often served him well—but Nick spoke so loudly he could have been inviting the entire line to his table, so John just nodded and mouthed "okay." He decided against the meatballs, filled his glass with some sticky looking orange liquid, and waited for Nick.

"Is that all you're eatin'?" Nick asked looking at John's plate. On Nick's plate was a small mountain of spaghetti and about twelve golf ball-sized meatballs. He had filled three glasses with lemonade. "I'll take as much as they'll give me," Nick said. "I'll burn it off later."

John assumed Nick was referring to his girlfriend's apartment, but judging by the size of his shoulders and chest, he might have meant on the practice field of just about any sport. Walking behind Nick toward an open table, John thought about how odd they must look together, this tall, scrawny bookworm and that solid, massive athlete. Surely, they'd have nothing in common. John was dreading every moment. What in the world were they going to talk about?

He needn't have worried.

"So how d'ya like it so far, John? Any good classes? Man, I'll tell ya, some of the women around here! It's a good thing my girlfriend's here. I love it when it's this warm out. Another two months, they'll all be covered in flannel. Of course when it's this hot I hate practice, but we should be real good this year. You play anything? Soccer's my sport. Baseball, too."

Nick went on like this for a solid ten minutes, all the while, sucking spaghetti noodles and eating whole meatballs. The entire time, John could think of only one question. When Nick finished eating and paused to wipe sauce from his chin, John asked him: "What's your girl-friend's name?" He braced himself, half expecting for some inexplicable reason to hear "Eileen O'Neill" filtered through the napkin at Nick's lips.

Having just covered several hundred topics and raised just as many possible questions, Nick must have been shocked at this one, but he answered quickly and with a hint of a smile, "Jennifer Wiener, and no hot dog or any other jokes or I'll kill ya."

*Oh my God,* John thought, *It's her—Wiener, Party of Eight.* But he was too relieved to laugh. "Jennifer Wiener? I think she's in my writing class. The professor called her Jennifer Whiner."

"She might be—in your class, I mean," Nick said. "She failed a couple a classes last semester. She's not dumb. She just doesn't express herself well. I told her I'd help her this semester now that I'm here."

*Yeah, right,* John said to himself. Aloud he asked "What's your major?"

"Elementary education. I'm minoring in psychology. How about you? I know everyone says I won't get a job, but I wouldn't want to major in anything else. I'll start my own school if I have to."

John wasn't sure whether he was still expected to answer. "I haven't decided. Communications or English."

"What do you want to do?"

"Write."

"Like, for a newspaper?" Nick asked.

"Maybe. I haven't really thought it out yet. I..."

Nick interrupted him. "Hey, John, check this guy out." John appreciated the camaraderie in Nick's tone. He turned around in his chair.

While pretty much every male student in the cafeteria was dressed in the same outfit—cap, tee shirt, shorts or baggy jeans, sandals or sneakers—"this guy" was dressed in a full double-breasted suit. *Jeez,* John thought, *this guy's taking college seriously.*

John didn't really care about the different mode of dress, but he thought it was best to play along. "He's probably some super brain or accounting major," John said.

Nick launched into a long discourse on how he once considered majoring in something like accounting but changed his mind when his sister had a baby who he loved to play with and teach new things and how that convinced him that he wanted to major in education and how he couldn't wait to get into a classroom preferably the early grades though he'd heard that some elementary education majors end up in sixth and seventh grade where the students couldn't care less about learning and he didn't want to waste his time on derelicts and wannabe drug addicts. Ending that free association of thoughts, Nick drained the last of his three glasses, stood up and said, "Well, Roomie, I guess I'll see you later."

"See ya, Nick."

As Nick walked away from the table John watched several girls at the next table nodding toward Nick's massive back and leaning in toward one another to whisper. He thought of Eileen, who he knew wasn't thinking of him.

# Thursday, August 28

Professor Watkins decided on Thursday to wait outside his classroom as his students entered. He hoped to reinforce the nice-guy image he had left them with on Tuesday. "Good Morning!" "How are you?" "What d'ya say?" "Good morning!" Some students returned his greeting; some grunted or nodded; some seemed surprised; some ignored him. In the classroom at nine a.m. he called roll and, relieved to find that the population of his classroom was lessened by only one, he good-naturedly tried to loosen up the remaining nineteen with a little banter: "I saw in this morning's paper that job prospects for college students look good over the next several years. The writer said that many business executives are advising college students to work on their communications skills, especially their writing, to help improve their chances of getting work."

Nothing. From the looks on their faces, Watkins guessed that they either did not care or had died of joy at the good news. He was trying to tell them that all the hard work they were going to do would pay off, that they didn't know it now, but they'd be thanking him in ten years when they were being appointed vice presidents and earning six-figure salaries and saving the planet because he'd taught them to write. To himself he said, *They think I'm all that stands between them and 10:15. Can't they see that I have their best interest at heart?* They weren't buying it.

It occurred to him to try a reference to sports or music, but he didn't want to risk trying to appear cool this early in the semester. It was better to be outrageously uncool, and therefore endearing and unthreatening, than to give the impression of *trying* to be cool. He returned to the first topic. "The writer went on to say that although fashionable majors will be in demand, so will the old-fashioned ones, like English and history. That's probably good news for some of you." A few shrugs. A slight nod or two. An indifferent raising of the eyebrows.

"OK," he said, "How did you all make out on the writing exercise?"

"I didn't know what you were looking for?"

"What exactly did you want on that?"

"I couldn't get started."

"I didn't really understand the question."

"Do we have to hand this in?"

"I couldn't get two-hundred words."

"Will you be grading these?"

Watkins was a bit dismayed, but not surprised. For the next half hour, he discussed their anxieties and expectations and talked for some time about finding their voices and freeing themselves from the fear of being evaluated and censured. He told them that no matter how many words they'd written, there was probably some marvelous jewel of an idea buried in their writing, an idea that could become an entire essay. He arranged the students in groups of four, asking them to share their ideas and help each other find the gems hidden in their exercises.

After twenty minutes of letting them discuss their writing (Watkins knew that most of the conversations had little to do with writing or diamond mining, but he hoped that the group discussions would allow the students to become acquainted and comfortable with one another), he assured them once again that there were treasures buried in their work, and to further prove it, he asked them to hand in their exercises, promising to return them on Tuesday after commenting in the margins on what was precious and rare. He listened to the zip of pages being torn from spiral bindings, collected the papers, placed them carefully in his briefcase, and dismissed the class.

Watkins returned to his office to prepare his afternoon section of English 100. At just after 3:00 he drove straight to his apartment, eager to begin reading his students' work, curious to learn who they were, desperate to get the assignments finished so they wouldn't interfere with his weekend. It wasn't that he disliked reading student prose; in fact, he often found it interesting, humorous and rewarding. But just as often, student writing could be tiresome, uninspired, abstract, cliché-ridden, and just plain boring. Students sometimes seemed to forget, Watkins realized, that a real-life human being—who liked as much as anyone else to be entertained, thrilled, and challenged—would read what they wrote.

At his apartment, Watkins flipped quickly through his mail to see if Diane had responded to his last letter and, finding nothing but bills and advertisements, sat on the futon and instinctively picked up the remote.

On the small, used television his sister had given him—*I really should thank her*, he thought. *I never call her*—he surfed through the afternoon talk shows, game shows and soap operas, past the gardening and cooking instructions, paused for a few moments at a Jewel video he was tired of, and settled on the sports channel, airing the start of a rare day game, this one between the Phillies and Astros, two teams Watkins cared little for primarily because he couldn't stand to watch baseball on plastic grass. Turning off the television, he pulled his briefcase toward him and took out the stack of writing assignments.

"My name is Jennifer Wiener. I am nineteen years old. I was born in 1978. My parents are Edward and Martha Wiener. I am a student at Wexford College." Watkins set the paper down, turned on the television to see how the Phillies were doing, watched an inning and decided to get back to work—*okay, after one more inning, just one more.* In the bottom of the eighth with the Astros ahead by fifteen runs, Watkins decided to return to his essays after a cup of coffee to help wake him up. He finished his coffee, watered his plant, shaved, called his sister, and cleaned the bathroom. With nothing to distract or entice him, he returned to Jennifer's essay: "Where I am a travel agency management major." *Travel agency management?* thought Watkins, then recalled that the school had introduced a whole range of new programs to attract more students. He suddenly remembered that he had not even begun to think about his Christmas shopping, and here it was September already.

### John

GROUPS! The word struck John like a punch to the chest. After overworking some metaphor about buried treasure and jewels, Watkins had so very casually commented that he wanted to divide the class into groups, apparently without considering for even a moment that this plan of his was like pouring a six-foot thick concrete slab over John's treasure island of buried ideas. John's breath came in short gasps and his stomach knotted. The rest of the class seemed to disappear in a haze. Even Eileen evaporated from his consciousness. No one had said anything about groups. It wasn't part of the school's advertising. It wasn't mentioned in the view book or college catalogue. It wasn't on the syllabus. It wasn't even hinted at on Tuesday. In his mind, John glared at Watkins and wished him dead.

But Watkins survived and continued his assault on the neat rows of desks and the emotional stability of his students. John could now concur with the assessment of Watkins—this dude was indeed nuts— offered on the first day of class by the student who was today part of his group, along with two students from the row directly in front of him. The four of them exchanged their papers counter-clockwise, and John began to read his classmate's writing.

"I'm supposed to write about 200 words on who I am for this class. I'm not sure what I'm supposed to write but here goes."

The "200" was crossed out and replaced with the words "two hundred." John read on, surprised at the errors in spelling and grammar, but even more astonished at the fact that although the writer's pen had started running out of ink at around the fiftieth word, the writer had nonetheless pressed onward, leaving on the page a barely visible trace of ink that became completely illegible by the end of the paragraph. In an effort to make the pen produce ink, the student had muscled the pen into the paper as he went along, with the result that the impressed words could be better felt than read.

He next read a neatly typed, freely associated autobiography from a student who grew up in a large city and was already finding life in this small town boring and uneventful. "I'm used to excitement," she wrote, listing the concerts, restaurants, shows, sporting events and boyfriends that had enlivened her summer.

The final piece, still in its notebook, contained a long list of this writer's connection to various groups, organizations, and classifications: Catholics, New Yorkers, Irish, youth groups, sports teams, honor societies, and clubs. She listed her age, race, gender, economic status, birthplace, high school GPA, height and eye color. It was like reading a person's driver's license and all the other documents in her wallet, John thought. It was like reading a living obituary.

When each group member had read the writing of the other three, they sat in silence for a few moments. Finally Jeremy spoke, "I really like the one about not having anything to do. I agree. This town sucks. There's not even a movie theatre."

"That was mine," said Belinda proudly.

"I liked that one, too," Meagan assured her.

John thought he should speak. It appeared to be his turn. Without averting his eyes from his paper and in a non-threatening tone, he asked them, "Why'd you come here?"

Belinda didn't hesitate: "My parents wanted me to, like, find a small college that wasn't too far away from them and where I wouldn't be, like, you know, too distracted. I wanted to go to State. This was, you know, their idea of, like, a compromise. You can't get smaller than this. My friends never even , like, heard of this place."

The three of them continued to bemoan the lack of entertainment in town and eventually moved on to other topics, while John sat quietly, relieved that someone else carried the weight. Finally, after what was surely an entire hour, Watkins rescued him, talked a little more about gemstones, collected the papers and dismissed the class. John gathered his belongings and looked toward his left to see Eileen leaving the room flanked by two guys hitting on her, John was certain. Another knockout punch. This was just not his day.

### *Watkins*

Watkins returned to his apartment after a few hours of browsing in *the* local record store and *the* local bookstore. *God*, he thought, *there isn't much to do in this town.* He returned with a Van Morrison CD he'd been meaning to buy and a book by Barbara Kingsolver and nothing for his family, which wasn't surprising since no one in his family listened to music or read books. This year would be no different from every other; starting around Labor Day, when the decorations went up at the malls, he would use the holiday as an excuse to shop in stores that interested him, and on Christmas Day he'd sheepishly present his sisters and parents with department store gift certificates dated 12/24.

He placed the CD in the stereo and began reading, stopping after a few pages with the same reaction he always had to truly good writing: he hated it because it reminded him by contrast of his own lousy writing skills, and he felt guilty for not doing something related to his work. He put down Kingsolver and picked up Wiener: "Someday I hope to be the manager of a travel agency. I love to travel. I went to Florida for senior week and I just loved it. I had a great time with all of my friends, who by the way are a various group." The paragraph went on like this, mercifully, for only another hundred words or so. But smack in the middle of the abstractions and repetitions was this sentence: "Mostly I want to travel because I can't wait to get out of here."

At first Watkins thought of telling Jennifer that a travel agency manager probably did more managing than traveling, but he confined himself to commenting on the feelings hinted at in that sentence. "Where's 'here'?" he wrote. "Why do you want to get out?" "What emotions led you to write this sentence?" Watkins suggested that thinking about why she wrote the sentence might help her discover who she was.

He moved on to the next student, and the next, and the next. As he predicted, while some of the writing bored him, much of it fascinated and inspired him. While some of what he read had been produced merely to fulfill the assignment, more of it revealed imagination, insight, fear, desperation, hope, compassion, pain and joy. The 4000 words typed, handwritten or word processed onto all manner of paper that now lay in Professor Watkins's lap provided a glimpse into the lives of nineteen rare individuals with a few characteristics common to their generation and many unique to themselves. One paper in particular reminded Watkins of why he became a teacher.

> Everyday when I am at work or school I worry about my grandmother. She sits in front of the TV all day long and watches talk shows or soap operas or whatever is on. She doesn't care or even change the channel if something is on that she doesn't like. She just sits there and sometimes cries. She used to be very active and went to church and had friends. But when her daughter died she lost it all. Her daughter was my mother and I loved her very much too and I miss her everyday. But I don't have time to be sad anymore. I have to take care of my little sister because my grandmother is too depressed to help me. When my father comes home from work he tries to help out, but he is too tired. And he is a lousy cook anyway. And he is still sad. My mother died about three years ago and when I go to bed I still sometimes hear my father crying in his bedroom. He is a good man and a good father but he doesn't help me much. I don't want to *be* a mother anymore. I want to *have* a mother.

With the back of his wrist, Watkins wiped the corner of his eye. He looked again at the writer's name and started to write a comment: "Eileen, This is . . . " He couldn't find the words to express how moving and honest the writing was, how touching without being maudlin.

He wanted to say how sorry he was and how her words had touched him. *What do I say*, he thought, *that won't sound stupid?* Words having failed the writing teacher, he crossed out "This is" and wrote instead "Please see me."

Watkins walked into his tiny kitchen and stared for a few moments at last night's greasy pizza box still sitting on the counter. He returned to his living room and dialed his mother's phone number.

"Hello."

"Hello, Ma."

"Petey!" she squealed, then lowered her voice a few octaves. "I mean 'Dr. Watkins.'" Then, nervously, "What's wrong?"

"Nothing. I just wanted to say hello."

"On a Thursday afternoon in the middle of the day? Something's wrong. I can hear it in your voice."

"Nothing's wrong," Watkins insisted, knowing that if this line of conversation continued he'd have to confess or make something up. "I just wanted to see how you're doing and tell you how my first week of class has been going."

"Oh, that's right. You started school this week."

"Yeah. It's funny how we all say that. People say that to me— 'When do you start school?' as if I'm six years old."

"Well, you'll always be six to me, Petey."

He should have seen that coming. "Okay, Ma. How's Dad?"

The conversation continued in the same vein for another fifteen minutes—no revelations, no discoveries, no significant observations, just the bonding of small talk and the necessary periodic reinforcement of love and affection. Watkins hung up the phone and, a bit rejuvenated, picked up the Kingsolver book and read a page. *God, I'm a lousy writer*, he thought, but flipped the page anyway.

### Eileen

GROUPS! The word struck Eileen like a gentle breeze. She loved meeting people, and the more different they were from her the better she enjoyed their company and ideas. She had taken the same seat on Thursday that she had selected in the first class, and at Watkins's first mention of groups she turned without waiting for any more encouragement or instruction to face the student on her right. They were

26

joined by another, the odd number of students in the class leaving their group with only three.

When they exchanged papers, Eileen read with great delight the words of her classmates, one of whom, Gary Kardell, defined himself almost exclusively as an employee of a fast food restaurant, and another, Tony Falcone, who wrote primarily about the sports he played and his summer job helping his father, a housepainter. Finishing the second paper, she looked up to find her two classmates staring at her, and although she had become accustomed to the stares of young men, there was something very different in the eyes of these two.

"I'm really sorry about your mother."

"Yeah, me too. That must have been awful."

Their sad looks and the sincerity in their voices affected Eileen deeply, and she struggled to shift the focus from herself. "You seem to be good at a lot of sports, Anthony."

"Yeah, I really enjoy playing sports. Was your mother young?"

"She was 45."

"How'd she die?"

"Car accident."

"God, that's awful, just awful," Gary said shaking his head lightly.

Despite her efforts to change the subject, her new friends continued to ask questions about the loss of Eileen's mother. Knowing that their questions were motivated by curiosity borne of kindness, sympathy and a bit of gratitude for their own good fortune, Eileen obligingly answered the questions of her classmates and assured them that she was dealing well with her ordeal.

When Watkins dismissed the class, Gary and Tony walked with Eileen out of the classroom, Tony just staring at Eileen and as if he couldn't comprehend being a motherless child, Gary continuing to sum up his feelings: "Just awful," he murmured, "just awful."

The sincerity and tenderness of her new friends buoyed Eileen's spirits, and she resolved to continue attending class. *It'll help me to get out of the house every once in a while*, she reasoned, getting into her car for the short drive home. By habit she flipped on the radio, still tuned to the same station:

"I'm Catholic and my fiancée is Jewish, but he's not very religious," the caller declared.

"Until the kids come along," Dr. Sally retorted.

"Sorry?"

"When you have kids, his religious fires will begin burning, and then there'll be trouble."

"But I'm sure he'll let me raise the children Catholic. He said so."

Sally was adamant: "No, he won't. You won't have a good marriage unless he converts. In fact, you can't have a good marriage with a member of a different religion because you'll be missing the strong spiritual bond necessary for a lasting marriage. Marriages need more than love to survive. And marriages between two people of different religions or different political philosophies or different races, for that matter, are not going to last. If you're religious and he's not, or you're Christian and he's Jewish, one of you is going to have to change. The children will suffer the consequences of having two such different parents. You'll want to take them to Mass; he'll want them to go to synagogue.

"Well, I'm not very religious myself. I mean, I do consider myself a good Christian. I just don't go to Mass every Sunday.

"Then you're not Catholic."

"Yes, I am," the caller insisted.

"Being Catholic means being a member of the religious family *and* practicing the tenets of your faith. You can't be Catholic unless you embrace all of the teachings of Christ as part of your daily living. Being Catholic means to live with the values and morals taught in the faith. To be Catholic, you must attend Mass every Sunday. Period."

"But just because I don't go to Mass on Sunday doesn't mean I'm not Catholic."

"Well," Sally responded, retreating slightly, "You're not a good Catholic."

The doctor declared herself the winner of that argument by announcing quickly that she had to break for commercials. Normally, Eileen reached for the control dial at the first mention of advertising, but she was slow on the draw and the announcer's first words caught her attention:

"Are you lonely? Tired of sitting home on Friday nights watching reruns or rented movies? Do you find yourself worrying about growing old without the security, comfort and companionship that only a long-time partner can provide? Then maybe the MateFind Dating Service is just what you're looking for."

Eileen wished it were as simple as the announcer implied in his smooth transition from a gloomy, suicidal tone to cheery optimism as he went on to describe the candle-lit dinners and moonlight walks that awaited clients of MateFind—*whose imaginations apparently extend no further than romance novels*, thought Eileen. She thought for a moment about her father, and then about herself. As lonely as she was, she wasn't ready to appeal to a dating service. Her mother had warned her years ago that her good looks might intimidate men or that men might assume she was unavailable. She looked in the rearview mirror. *Maybe I should do the asking.* She thought about Tony Falcone.

She listened to a few more commercials and a news report—a nineteen year old woman attending her high school prom had given birth in the bathroom, put the newborn in a garbage can, and returned to the ballroom, where she danced with her boyfriend and even requested a song from the band. Amazed and horrified, Eileen recalled the story of two high school students who had recently killed their hours-old child and tossed him into a dumpster, and the story of a young woman who drowned her two sons by strapping them into their car seats and pushing the car into a lake. Eileen punched the radio buttons, searching for something to distract her.

When she arrived home, she found her grandmother in her usual spot staring blankly at a television talk show, this one featuring two women, the son of one having killed the son of the other. Apparently eager to see more bloodshed, the host was intensifying the women's emotion with antagonistic questions: "Your son received a life sentence, Mrs. Walker. Don't you think he should have been given the death penalty? After all, he committed this murder deliberately."

"Well, yes, it was deliberate, but he felt his life was in danger because of the constant threats that Samuel made against him. Even in the bar that night, Samuel was swearing he'd get him someday. And, no, of course I don't want to see him executed. I realize he will be in jail for the rest of his life. I think that's punishment enough."

"How about you, Mrs. Gorshinski? Shouldn't Jackie die for what he did to your little Samuel?"

"Of course he should die. Fry him good. He killed my son. What kinda message are we sending young people in this country? That it's okay to just kill other people? We need to put these people to death. We can't have 'em walking the streets killing everybody in sight. The Bible says 'an eye for an eye.' That's good enough for me."

Though she opposed capital punishment, Eileen could appreciate the powerful emotions, even the vengeance, that governed Mrs. Gorshinski's thinking. "What do you think, Nana?" Eileen asked.

"About what?"

"Nothing important. How are you feeling today?"

"Fine, Dear. How was class?"

"Interesting. I think I might actually enjoy it. I have to clean a little down here today. Care to help me a bit?"

Asking for her help in cleaning the house was sometimes the only thing that would activate her grandmother, primarily because it conjured memories of happier times, Eileen realized, for often while they dusted and swept, polished and mopped, her grandmother would call her by her mother's name.

"Oh, I'd love to," Nana said, pushing herself up from her chair.

"Let's start in the kitchen."


### John

John walked slowly to his dorm, thinking about class, about Eileen's flirtatious new boyfriends, about the homework he had for his Friday classes, and about the bathroom. In his three days away from home, he had begun to adjust fairly well to having a roommate, hearing shouts and thuds at all hours of the night, being bombarded by everyone else's taste in music, and experiencing hourly the sights, sounds and smells that came with living among other young men. But the one thing he hadn't learned in his eighteen years of living in relative solitude at home was how to share a bathroom with strangers. He tried to time his visits to insure privacy, but he usually discovered that at least one other equally hypermodest person had come to that solution moments before he had. This was serious. As a young boy of maybe eight or nine, he had visited an army barracks with his cub scout troop. Horrified to discover that the stalls in the men's room had no doors, he determined at that moment that even if the United States were under attack on all sides, he absolutely would refuse to join the army. The risk of getting killed was a distant second reason.

He rode the elevator to his floor and, walking toward his room, paused outside the bathroom door. Hearing nothing from within, he slipped inside, checked for feet, and, moving as if someone were sleeping in the same room, quietly slid into a stall and began laying toilet paper out on the seat—another of his mother's many safety measures. No sooner had his bottom hit the seat when—Bang!—the bathroom door flew open with tremendous force. John stood up, unrolled a bit of paper and tossed it in the toilet, flushed, buttoned, zipped, buckled and opened the stall door.

"Johnny, buddy!" Nick said with overwhelming enthusiasm and turned again to face the wall. "What's up? Hey, you wanna do something after classes today? Shoot some baskets, maybe? Toss around the baseball? We could get a few other guys from the floor and play a little street hockey."

John quickly reviewed his mental picture of their room. *Baseball glove, basketball, hockey stick, football, ping pong paddles, skis, volley ball, racquetball racquet, lawn darts.   What* doesn't *Nick have?* "I really don't like to play many sports. Tennis is actually my game," he lied.

"Sounds good. We'll play around four o'clock. The school's got great courts. There should be one available around four."

"Oh, but I, uh . . . I didn't bring my racquet."

"No problem. Jen's got a racquet you can use. In fact, she's got mine." Nick zipped up. "I'll go get them after class this afternoon and meet you back in the room." He left without waiting for a response.

John spent the remainder of the day trying to invent a plausible excuse. *Tennis?! Why tennis? What a fool! Why didn't I think of swimming? Swimming is my sport from now on.*

At a quarter after four Nick exploded into the room.

"We should probably try to move that desk and chair somewhere else," John offered in a tone he hoped made clear that he was exonerating Nick and blaming the furniture for being in an inconvenient location. John knew no rearrangements were possible. The room seemed to have been built around the furniture, which fit together like puzzle pieces.

"Yeah, I guess," Nick said. "Are you ready? You sure you want to play in those clothes? How you gonna run in jeans? Shouldn't you put on a pair of sneaks? Are you sure you played tennis before?"

"I really hadn't planned on playing," John answered, "so I didn't bring my stuff. Since the surgery, I haven't been able to play. It's very difficult for me to control a racquet with so much ligament damage in my wrist."

Nick was astonished. "You didn't say anything about surgery before. What surgery?"

John went on to explain how he landed on his wrist while diving for a ball during the finals of the district championship in his senior year. Although he won the point and the match, he added, he lost the use of his right hand for months and ended a promising career, at least in collegiate tennis.

"You can't even see any scars on your wrist," Nick noted.

"It's amazing what they can do these days with lasers," John responded. "If only they could have returned it to its full use. Ah, well."

"Do you still want to play?"

"Oh sure," John said casually; "I could just help you practice your serve or something."

To John's surprise, Nick agreed, although John perceived little enthusiasm in his voice.

*       *       *

"You're standin' a little close, John. You don't think I can serve, do you?"

"Let's see what you got."

What Nick had was a rifle shot that hit deep in the service box and afforded John little time to send the panic signal from his brain all the way to his right hand, where he held the racquet like a crossing guard with a stop sign. The ball skipped off the court and plunked John solidly in the thigh above his right knee.

"Not bad, hey, John?" Nick said amiably.

"No, not bad at all," John responded backing toward the base line. "Was that a once-in-a-lifetime shot?"

*Ok, twice*, John thought as Nick's second serve rocketed past him three feet to his left. Quick as a rabbit, but ridiculously uncoordinated, he lunged at the ball and stumbled forward, frantically trying to save himself from falling on his face. He could hear the loud slapping of his sandals on the hard surface of the court as he struggled to move his legs quickly enough to catch the bottom half of his body up with the top half, which now plunged headlong toward the fence. When he finally straightened, he looked at Nick, staring at John in disbelief.

"You okay, John?"

"Yeah, it's been a while. I've lost my court sense, I guess."

"You wanna quit?"

"Nah. I'm sure I'll get back into it eventually."

John spent the next half hour using his stop sign to protect his face and groin from Nick's fireballs and making a game of the situation by periodically saying *Ha, missed me* to himself. After each time Nick had served the six balls he'd brought, John would collect them and return each by dropping it and swinging his racquet. He'd then walk to the net, pick up the two or three that had made it only that far, and finish the job of returning them to Nick.

Walking back to their room, Nick asked John how his wrist was.

"Oh, fine, thanks."

"You never played tennis before, did you?"

"What was your first clue?" John responded with a slight grin.

"And your wrist?"

"I can't think of anything I've ever done to even endanger it let alone tear it up."

"Why did you lie to me?" Nick asked, puzzled but clearly more concerned that he had been deceived by someone he had trusted.

John was startled at Nick's demeanor. In this situation he would have expected a brutal razzing full of vulgarity, slang and spit. Nick's maturity baffled John.

"I'm not sure. I didn't want you to think I was a geek with no athleticism."

"I'll think you're a geek if you say 'athleticism' again. I don't care if you can play tennis, or baseball or hockey or anything. Who gives a shit if you're a sports star or not? I'm sure we'll find something we can do together. You must do something besides read and write."

John brightened. "I like to play chess."

"Oh, sorry," Nick responded, "I can't think clearly enough to play chess since I banged my head off the edge of the table diving for a pawn that had fallen off the board during my match with Kasparov last year."

John laughed. The thought of having a friend excited and frightened him at the same time. He was thrilled at the prospect of having someone to talk to and nervous that he'd screw it up when he talked too much. "Touché," he said.

Nick was chuckling, too. "You know, Johnny Mariner, I think this is the beginning of a beautiful friendship. I always wanted to use that line. I wonder where it's from."

"It's from an old Humphrey Bogart movie, and I think you might be right."

"How'd you get so smart, Johnny Mariner? Not by watching old movies, I'll bet. Hey, what is your last name, anyway."

*Oh, no,* John thought, *Oh, no.* "Believe it or not, it's Mariner."

Nick squinted and cocked his head.

"It's Zajaczkiewicz," John said.

"Zines-kevitch," Nick replied, trying.

"Zajaczkiewicz."

"Ok, now we're getting somewhere, Johnny Mariner."

# Tuesday, September 2

Watkins spent his weekend evenings with a stack of rented movies and a half-case of Rolling Rock.  During the day, he prepared his classes for the coming week, finished the Kingsolver novel, washed the coffee mugs and silverware collecting in his sink, shopped for groceries, dreamt on Saturday night that he was late for class because he couldn't find the building, and bolted straight up in bed on Sunday morning believing that he had slept through his Monday morning literature class.

On Tuesday morning he awoke looking directly at the digits on his clock-radio: 8:40. *8:40! Jesus! Twenty minutes! I can't believe it.* He jumped from the bed. *No time to shower.* He pulled on his jeans, picked yesterday's shirt off the floor and, holding it to his nose, inhaled deeply. *Good enough.* He threw cold water on his face and slicked back his long hair. *Well, there'll be no hiding what happened,* he thought. *I can't believe this! The third class!* He grabbed his briefcase and ran to his car.

Watkins ran up the two flights of stairs in the Humanities Building and at approximately eight minutes past nine opened the classroom door.  The activity and buzzing in the room halted immediately and was replaced by a muted chorus of tsking sounds, groans, "*damns*," and "*shits*," clear signs that they all had moments before his arrival been praying fervently that he wouldn't show.

"I'm sorry I'm late.  I appreciate your patience."

"Rough night, Professor Watkins?  Long weekend?"

Stunned, Watkins looked at Theodore Crossings, knowing that this unorthodox comment could be interpreted in two ways.  Either Crossings was an arrogant snob using the occasion to gain a little leverage on him, or Crossings was reaching out to Watkins in a friendly gesture to lighten the moment.  He opted for the less paranoid interpretation, but his discomfort was stronger than his desire to return the frivolity.

"Well, I uh, I uh, no I had an okay night, an okay weekend.  I uh, I sometimes just, uh, sleep in."  He shrugged his shoulders and raised his eyebrows as if to add, "What more can I say?" and knew that his embarrassment was clear to everyone. "Anyway," he continued, "let's get on to the lesson." *I could have handled that a bit better,* he thought. *They probably think I'm a freak.*

He started by returning their exercises, calling their names aloud: "Albright, Jackson, Falcone, Jessica, Crossings, Kardell, O'Neill. Eileen O'Neill. Is Eileen here?" He held the paper out and turned so that everyone in the class had a chance of confessing to be Eileen O'Neill. Assuming he hadn't been as persuasive as he thought, Watkins placed her paper on the bottom of the stack and continued calling names.

He spent the hour talking about brainstorming—mapping an idea from the jewel they found—about finding a thesis, and about organizing a paper. When he dismissed them, he watched about half of them leave, while the other half approached the desk.

"Professor Watkins, I'm not sure I understand what you mean by this comment: 'The is a something in testing parades. I thick radar would something something more a boat something pope are defied by the wok the do.'"

Watkins took the paper from the student: "This is a very interesting paragraph. I think readers would enjoy hearing more about how people are defined by the work they do," he read. "I'm sorry, Gary," he continued, "my handwriting can be a bit sloppy. I do think you have an interesting idea here, about how working in a restaurant is such a part of your identity. The sentence about how scarred your arms are from hot grease is excellent, and I liked the part about how you even dream—or should I say have nightmares—about bagging fries. There's some good stuff here."

Gary appeared unaccustomed to hearing such praise. He mumbled a "thank you," took the paper, and, reading his own words, left the room.

"Professor Watkins, I want to say I didn't mean to give you a paper you couldn't read. I wrote it right before class and I had just the one pen and I didn't know you were going to collect it. Can I do it over?"

"Of course," Watkins said, "but try to give yourself enough time to do your work correctly. You can't learn to write if you wait until the last minute."

"Professor Watkins, I wasn't sure of what you wanted," the next student in line said plaintively. Watkins always laughed to himself

36

when asked this question, but he calmly explained that what he wanted had nothing to do with the student's ideas or her writing.

"Professor Watkins," the next student said, sounding very nervous and uncomfortable and looking down at his paper, "I, uh, know you said you weren't going to, uh, grade these exercises, but I was just wondering if you, uh, could just, uh, tell me what this would have gotten if you *were* grading it?"

Watkins reached into his pocket, took out a measure of rope, tied the end into a noose, and hanged himself.

### Eileen

Eileen's weekend passed like most others in the past two and half years, and on Tuesday morning, she sat on the edge of her little sister's bed, watching her sleep and thinking about the events of the past few days.

All weekend, she'd cleaned the house, cooked the meals, washed the dishes and the clothes, shopped, entertained her sister and helped her with her homework, nursed her grandmother, and helped her father come two days closer to regaining some degree of tranquility in his life. The family attended Mass on Sunday and afterwards went to breakfast at a nearby pancake restaurant that Maureen especially liked.

"I'm getting sausage, Dad. Is that okay," Maury asked.

"Of course it is, Sweetie. You get anything you like."

It was how the conversation started every Sunday, with her sister asking permission to order whatever she had a taste for that day and her father approving the request. He would have allowed his daughter to order an entire pig if she desired it. She didn't really need to ask, but Maury seemed unable to make a move without someone's approval, as if acting of her own volition would result in some catastrophe. Eileen often encouraged her sister to think for herself and to take risks, but at ten years old, Maury seemed more comfortable living within the confines of a life whose limits were determined by her father. Eileen didn't press her too hard on the issue; she knew that Maury was making her own peace with the world.

"Isn't Sheila here this morning?" her father asked the server when she came to the table.

"She's on vacation this week. I'll try to do as good a job as she does," she said pleasantly.

Eileen's father blushed slightly. "Why don't you go ahead, Maury." Eileen wondered how people seeing her family for the first time perceived them all—a young child, a teenage woman, a forty-five-year-old man who looked ten years younger, and an elderly woman whose sadness added ten years. Did others wonder what the relationships were? Did they think that her father had married a younger woman? She sometimes resisted the desire to detail her genealogy to strangers, but on occasion, she made certain to stress "my father" and "my sister" when introducing the family to others.

Sunday afternoon and evening passed quickly, and on Monday morning, Eileen was awakened at 6:00 by Maury calling from her bed, "Eileen, I don't feel good. Eileen! Ei . . !" Her name was stopped by a loud and familiar guttural sound as Maury threw up mostly over the side of the bed.

"Maury!" Eileen shouted and leapt from the bed. She half-carried, half-dragged Maury to the bathroom and held her head while Maury, crying and gasping, heaved into the toilet. After cleaning her up and changing the linen, Eileen put Maury back in bed.

"I'm sorry, Eileen."

She stroked Maury's hair. "Don't you dare apologize for that, Maury. You didn't do anything wrong. You're entitled to get sick. You feel a bit warm. Let me get a thermometer."

"Is everything okay?" Eileen's father asked from the doorway.

"She's fine, Dad."

He came into the room and sat on the edge of the bed. "You all right, Sweetie?"

"I'm sorry, Daddy."

"Well, you should be," he said. "Now I'm just going to have to feed you again tomorrow. You were supposed to make that food stay in there for a week, don't you know? What am I going to do with you?"

Wondering how they could be so lucky and unfortunate at the same time, Eileen left the room to look for a thermometer.

On Monday night Maury was not much better. "You're not going anywhere tomorrow, Honey. In fact, you might miss a few days this week. I'll go over to Sister Margaret to get your work so you don't get behind."

On Tuesday, Eileen stayed home from school as well and added "teacher" to the list of roles she played in the life of her family.

# *John*

Jen was already in her seat when John entered room 312 on Tuesday morning at a few moments before nine.

"Hi, John," she sang as he walked by. "Feeling better?"

John just grunted and found his seat. His first college weekend had not been pleasant. His first serious bout of homesickness prevented him from doing much more on Friday evening and Saturday than studying in his room and calling home. But the far-worse sickness that followed after his first serious bout of drinking left him swearing never to touch alcohol again as long as he lived, so help him God, never, never, never again. Actually he hadn't drunk *that* much, but it was more than he was used to, which was none, so even the fragrance of beer or the effervescence from a freshly poured glass gave him a head-start on everyone else. Three hours after he arrived at the party on Saturday night, his new best friends in all the world, Nick and Jen, were dragging him back to his room, where they stayed to keep an eye on him and a hand on each other.

John passed the night fitfully. He awoke with a tremendous headache after dreaming that Eileen O'Neill was teaching his writing class and that she kept insisting in a heavy Irish accent that John come to the front of the room to dance a jig and sing a song for everyone. He had just let out the first note when he awoke groaning out loud and drooling on the pillow.

Now it was three days later, and he was still feeling a bit toxic and not thinking very clearly. Jen turned around to face John, sitting three rows behind her: "Man, were you sick, John! I thought you might drown in your own barf." Several students turned to look at him. He thought for a moment that he should be enjoying this attention, that this was his chance to create for himself a heroic identity. In one week he could rise from nothing to become a legend, the Cinderella college kid trading the anonymity or disdain that scholarship brings for the notoriety and respect that comes with drunkenness and hangovers. Now was the time to transform himself: as a teenager, he could change costume in the middle of the act and no one would think it unusual. All weekend he'd taken note of the various means by which his companions established their individuality—the goatees, T-shirts, tattoos, work boots, lingo, jewelry, gestures, habits, hats and haircuts that were all part of the cultivation of personas at Wexford College. And among all of the efforts to be known as someone different, he'd noticed on Sunday at lunch and all day Monday that someone's drinking skills, drunken behavior and foggy half-consciousness the following morning were rewarded with chaffing tinged with admiration.

Recalling Sunday morning, John chose anonymity. He looked at Jen and said, "That was the last time."

She laughed. "I remember saying that, too, John," she replied.

At nine o'clock, the conversations in the room turned almost instantly to the topic of Watkins's absence. Everyone seemed to have an opinion on the matter:

"I'm sure he'll be here in a second. He seems pretty serious about starting on time."

"He's probably not taking a sick day. It's only the third class."

"Maybe he was in an accident."

"I had a teacher in high school who slept in just about everyday. He used to show up with the worst bed head."

"Maybe he quit."

"Maybe he's dead."

Several students laughed. "I hope he died before he read my assignment," one said.

"That's not funny," someone said. "He's just a young guy."

From another student: "How old do you think he is?"

"I'd say mid-thirties, maybe thirty-five."

"That old!" another exclaimed. "I'd guess more like thirty-one or so."

From yet another student: "I think he tries to dress young."

The debate over Watkins's age continued for a few minutes more, opinions being supported by evidence of Watkins's clothing, the poor shape he was apparently in, his mannerisms, and the verbal habits that had already begun to bug some students. Suddenly one student changed the subject.

"Hey, how long are we supposed to give him? I mean before we leave?"

"I say we leave now," someone said starting to stand but changing his mind when he saw no one was following his lead.

"It's only been five minutes. I think we're supposed to give him longer than that."

Jen, the veteran, set the matter straight: "He's new so he's probably an assistant professor. You give an assistant professor ten minutes. An associate professor gets fifteen. And a full professor gets twenty."

She announced this schedule so authoritatively that no one questioned her. *How does she know this stuff?* John wondered; *I didn't see this anywhere. And what's an assistant professor?*

"How do you know all that?" someone asked.

"It's common knowledge," Jen assured him.

"Well then he's got two minutes" came the response.

At that moment the door opened and Watkins appeared, looking as if someone had sprayed him full in the face with a garden hose. His hair was still wet and sweat ran down his temples.

"I'm sorry I'm late," he said. "I appreciate your patience."

John could hear a few muted notes of displeasure among his peers, but he knew that, like him, no one was really all that disappointed since no one actually expected Watkins to miss class. Then a most shocking development occurred when some student in the second row asked Watkins if he'd had a rough night. John was flabbergasted. *How could a kid be that familiar with a professor? How could he have the guts?* Everyone looked at Watkins. *How would he handle this?*

John thought Watkins dealt with it well. He didn't get angry or critical. Impressed with Watkins's demeanor, John waited to receive his corrected assignment. When Watkins mentioned Eileen O'Neill's name three times, John looked over at her empty chair, realizing for the first time that she was not there. He was grateful that she had not heard the "drowning in your own barf" comment. It was not an image he wanted her to have.

John took his paper from Watkins, turned immediately to the last page and by habit looked for a grade. *Oh, that's right, no grade on this,* he realized. He read Watkins's comment, which took some concentration:

> John,
>
> You obviously know how to write. What you've written here is very interesting, sophisticated, and well developed. Your writing is well-organized and coherent, and you even have a thesis sentence. Your vocabulary is very mature, and you vary your sentence structures throughout. You didn't

have to do so much for an exercise, but it's clear that you enjoy writing and that you are good at it.

Although this assignment as you've submitted it would serve as a paper, there are still a few ideas that you could develop and that could be the focus of another essay. Perhaps you could talk more about your father, the dangerous job he has, and how he has served to shape your thinking.

*Well* that's *not going to happen*, John thought. He was complimented by Watkins's comments and took great encouragement from them. But he was bothered by the lack of a grade. All through school he'd counted on the grade as a simple indicator of the worth of his work. In twelve years of education, he had come to expect an evaluation in quantifiable terms, and so he was more familiar with reading a single letter than with interpreting a number of sentences or paragraphs containing a professor's comments. And, being honest with himself, he needed to know that his work was "A" level, that Watkins approved entirely of his efforts.

For the remainder of the hour, John listened to Watkins, took notes, and listened to the class discussion, but he could not shake the need to know what his assignment had scored. When Watkins dismissed the class, John summoned every ounce—okay, *the* ounce—of his courage and approached Watkins to ask what grade his paper would have received.

He stammered his question. Despite the odd, pained look on Watkins's face, the professor gently affirmed his written evaluation, assured John that his work was superior, and admonished him to think less of grades and more about achieving the objectives of his writing. Watkins ended by startling John with a comment he could never have anticipated: "Besides," Watkins said, "there's more to college than grades."

# CHAPTER II

# *Tuesday, October 14*

## *John*

Watkins's words from more than a month ago echoed in John's mind as he sat on his bed looking at his midterm report for the general education classes he had selected for his first semester: Psychology: A, Math: A, History: A, Political Science: A, Composition: B+, a B+ in the course that would form the foundation of his major, a B+ in the subject he most enjoyed, a B+ in that bastard Watkins's class. Well there may be more to college than grades for some loser professor, but not for John Zajaczkiewicz. What did this guy want from him, anyway? He had submitted two essays and both had received the same grade, a B+. Maybe Watkins didn't give A's. No, he'd seen an A on another student's essay. Maybe Watkins favored girls. Couldn't be; Jen was getting C's. Maybe Watkins didn't really read the papers carefully, didn't like his style, didn't like him! That was probably it. Watkins didn't like John. *It's probably because I don't participate in class. Or I'll bet it goes back to that first day of class when he harassed me about my name. Maybe it's because I sit in the back. I'll bet it's because I sit in the back.* He was convinced.

Nick entered in his customary fashion, though the blow to the furniture had softened just a bit, primarily because the back of the desk chair had splintered and the softer wood absorbed the shock better.

"Hey, I recognize that slip of paper. How'd ya do? I did better than I thought I did. Four B's and a B+. A 3.1 GPA so far. Not bad, huh? I know, some people think a B's not so good, but I think a B is fine. I'm actually pretty happy with how I'm doin', though I want to do a bit better in my ed. classes when they start next semester. My parents are going to be thrilled. They worry sometimes that I'm more interested in sports and Jen than in studying, which is sometimes true, come to think of it."

"What did ya get the B+ in, Nick?" John asked.

"Composition."

That did it. John became more upset, but he whined his anger: "I don't understand why I can't do better in writing. That's my favorite subject. He told me at the beginning of the course that I was good at writing. I guess he changed his mind. I'm sitting up front from now on."

"What did you get?"

"A B+."

"Oh, a B+ is a bad grade? Screw you."

"I'm sorry, Nick. I don't mean it that way. It's just that Watkins doesn't like me, so I don't have a chance in this class. I never got less than an A- on my writing in high school.

"John, you are a first-class jerk. For someone so brilliant you really aren't too smart. First of all, you're acting as if you failed. Second, how do you know he doesn't like you? He doesn't even know you. I'm sure he doesn't give a shit for you. Just like me." He laughed. "Why don't you make an appointment with him and talk to him about your grade and your work? That's what I'd do."

"Well he's got the third one now, so maybe I'll wait and see if I do any better on that one. We had to write a cause and effect paper about problems we saw in our generation. He said he'd have them back by Thursday. If I get a B+, I'll go see him."

"You won't."

"I swear I will."

"Sounds like you're serious, but we'll see. In the meantime, what d'ya say we clean this room?"

John looked around. Just two weeks earlier he had taken his laundry home to his mother and had straightened the room. Now shirts, jeans, shorts, socks, and underwear lay everywhere. A half-eaten turkey sub sat like a paper weight on a stack of essays, hand-outs and notebooks that shared the desk with toothpaste tubes, de-odorant sticks, cologne bottles, encrusted cafeteria silverware, and a picture of Jen and Nick lying face down as if they'd both exhausted themselves from standing there for a month in their prom outfits. Nick's sports equipment lay wherever he had thrown it after a game or a season ended, and two of the three supermodels bent over into the room, the adhesive tape on their upper halves having loosened under the weight somewhere near the end of September. Neither bed was made, of course, but these beds were *really* not made. The sheets were balled up with the blanket and pillow, making it appear that anyone who would have slept in either bed would have awak-ened in the middle of a cloth cocoon. Not one dresser drawer was fully closed, and neither, it seems, was any book. They lay in various parts of the room, all set cover-up with the pages spread to mark the spot where their reader grew bored or got distracted. Computer disks lay on the floor and on top of the dresser, but atop the stereo sat a small stack of compact disks, the neat, sharp corners appearing very out of place in the shabby room made soft by so many scattered clothes.

John picked up the only CD cover not on the stack, took the CD out of the stereo, placed it in the cover, and set it gently and squarely on top of the others.

"Good job," said Nick. "Let's eat."


### Eileen

"Not at all, dear," Eileen's grandmother said when asked if she minded some music while they cleaned the living room. Eileen put on one of her favorites, Hootie's *Cracked Rear View*. She knew that Hootie had fallen out of fashion, but she nonetheless still enjoyed the music, and some of the songs spoke to her personally. She turned the volume to a level she knew wouldn't upset her grandmother and together they continued their thorough purification of the house, working methodically and diligently. Her grandmother would tolerate no corner-cutting. Eileen dusted the tops of the pictures, under the lamps, under every ornamental object on the coffee table and end tables. As they worked, Eileen hummed and sang softly to herself. With the dusting finished, they vacuumed the upholstered furniture, then moved it all to vacuum underneath.

Hearing the mail carrier on the porch, Eileen went outside. She opened the only envelope addressed to her and found nothing in the report surprising—a B in Literature and no grade in writing. She owed Watkins the second essay from several weeks ago, an essay in which she was expected to illustrate something about the current members of her family. She had found it impossible to write.

"What did you get in the mail, honey?" her grandmother asked when she shut off the vacuum.

"My mid-term grades."

"And how did you do?"

"I got a B in Literature," Eileen said enthusiastically.

"Oh, that's very good. Your mother would be proud. She was a good reader, too, you know." Eileen sometimes got the impression that her grandmother didn't truly understand what college work entailed, and her comments often suggested to Eileen that she saw little difference between reading a Harlequin Romance and a Romantic poem. Eileen's mother, who loved modern romance novels, had not gone to college. In fact, Eileen was the first in the family.

"Why didn't you go to college, Nana?"

"Me!" Nana responded, seemingly shocked. "Oh, I could never have afforded it, and besides, girls like me didn't go to college in those days. We would have been lucky if one of the boys had went. No, we weren't college people." She bent down and unplugged the vacuum cord.

"What do you mean 'girls like you'?"

"You know, girls that come from worker's families. I went to high school and worked at the recycling center for two years till your granddad come back. Then we got married and I had your uncle and your mother. College! It wouldn't have ever crossed my mind!"

"Are you sorry you didn't go?"

"No!" she replied in a tone that also said "Don't be silly." "I was a good wife and a good mother. I didn't need to go to school to boil your granddad's dinner or sew your mother's dresses."

The last few words were slow in coming, and Eileen knew that her grandmother, who had endured too much sadness, would begin to find the conversation torturous if it remained personal. She quickly changed course. "So, women didn't go to college?"

"Well, some did. Two or three from high school went to the teacher's college, and a couple went to nursing school and some to a fancy girl's college." She finished winding the vacuum cord around its hooks and wheeled the vacuum into a closet. "But, you know, it was rare to send girls to college in them days. You know, they might learn a thing or two and get carried away with themselves, and then they'd be looking to work in the banks and lawyer's offices—and not just taking dictation. Probably runnin' the place. Can't have that, now can we?"

Eileen was certain—maybe just hopeful—that she detected a hint of sarcasm in her grandmother's voice. "It's a different world today, isn't it, Nan?"

"Oh my, sometimes I think we moved so fast I can't keep up."

Eileen like the sound of the first person in her grandmother's sentence. "By 'we' you mean 'we women'?"

"I guess I do," her grandmother responded, sounding surprised at what she had apparently revealed. "Yes, we women. But don't get me wrong, now. I don't think one's better'n the other. The dear God who loveth us, he made and loveth *all*. Every living thing should be treated with respect, and a woman is a living thing. Women, the same as men, deserve kindness. No one's better. I'm no femininist," she said. Eileen didn't correct her.

With the cleaning finished, Eileen knew that her grandmother would settle into an afternoon of almost catatonic television watching. Unable to persuade her to continue the conversation, Eileen sat next to her on the couch and watched along. When the talk-show host introduced her first guest, Eileen was startled to see the face behind a voice she'd heard many times. "Hey, Nana," she exclaimed, "that's the woman from the radio, the one Mom used to listen to. I hear her every once in a while in the car. She's awful." Her grandmother didn't respond. Eileen assumed her mind was elsewhere.

"Welcome to the program, Doctor," the host said cordially. "It's great to have you here. You're like the Frasier of real radio."

"A lot of people make that comparison, which is okay with me as long as they realize I'm not a fictional character."

"And Frasier doesn't get the criticism you do. You've been taking a lot of heat in the liberal mainstream press lately."

"People are welcome to disagree with anything I say," the doctor responded. "I just hope they do so in a civilized manner. Attacking me personally for my opinions is hardly an intelligent argumentative strategy."

"Some misguided critics say that you attack people personally. You call them names. You berate them for the choices they've made."

"That's a matter of opinion. Most of my listeners would disagree with the assertion that I attack anyone."

"You called a listener a 'slut' once," the host replied. "I heard you do it."

"Well, calling you—I mean *someone*—calling *someone* (the audience laughed) a slut if she is one is not an attack. It's the truth, and sometimes the truth hurts. That's why some people condemn me. They don't like to hear the truth. People who resist the truth often become hostile. But getting back to your original comment, I do not like to be attacked personally mainly because it's not a healthy way to argue a point."

"I couldn't agree more with you. You tell it like it is, and people who can't face life honestly criticize you for your honest statements. But as someone who dispenses advice, aren't you open to attack, especially if someone can point to inconsistencies between what you say and what you do? After all, someone might claim that that's hypocrisy?" The interrogator was so good-natured about this question that she seemed to be equating hypocrisy with other "no-no's" like going out on a cold day with wet hair.

"I don't think so. But, first, let me make clear that I do not advise people about what they *should* do. I merely state my convictions and perhaps encourage listeners to make the choices I would make. And I believe that a person can make mistakes in her life and still have an opinion that doesn't gel with her previous actions. Sometimes we learn from our mistakes."

"So you're trying to prevent others from making the mistakes you made?"

"I'm trying to get people to take responsibility for their own lives, to get them to stop blaming everything and everybody else and to see that they make their own choices and that choices have consequences."

"Oh, aren't you tired of it?" The interviewer was fully on board now. "People today seem incapable of accepting the aftermath of their actions. Everyone's a victim," she said sarcastically. "No one seems to realize that they and they alone are responsible for who they are, what they do, what happens to them, and what they become. Stop whining and grow up, for heaven's sake."

The audience cheered wildly.

"You are so right," the guest assured her. We need to get back to a time when we taught children that they will be held accountable for what they do. I had a caller one time tell me that she came home one day to find her neighbor's son—he was about thirteen—in her home. The young man had broken in and was sleeping in one of the upstairs beds. This woman wanted to know if she should tell the parents! Can you imagine! When I was a young girl, if I did something like that, no one would ask if my parents should be notified. They'd be told, and I'd be disciplined. It just doesn't happen these days. We're too worried about the child's 'self-esteem.'"

· "You think parents need to be more involved in their children's lives?"

"Oh, absolutely. We would have far fewer problems in this country—less crime, fewer teen pregnancies, less drug abuse and gang violence—if more mothers stayed at home to raise their children."

Eileen got up and left the room.

# Thursday, October 16

12:15 a.m.  Watkins sat at his desk—a hollow core door he'd laid across two short filing cabinets—with a pencil in his right hand and his chin resting in the other.  He looked at his plant, struggling to hang on to its four remaining leaves.  "I think you drowned it," his mother told him during their last phone conversation.  Now he felt the same way.  Under the delusion that setting a deadline for himself would somehow force him to grade his essays on time, Watkins had promised his students that he'd return their papers during Thursday's class.  He took another mouthful of coffee and counted the number of papers remaining—ten, and all of them in the 9:00 section.  He had planned—as usual—to do the morning essays first so that when he had procrastinated until what was now *the* day the papers were to be returned, he could go to bed knowing that he'd have time between his two classes to finish grading.  Now he had no choice.  He could, of course, simply apologize and make the students wait until Tuesday, but he couldn't stand the thought of hearing them all groan at once, and he knew that no matter what he did for the rest of the semester, that collective groan would show up on the evaluation: "He never hands back the work on time."  Calling in sick wasn't an option.  He could say he had finished the papers but forgot to bring them so that he would appear to have kept his promise—sort of.  Or he could just press on and finish the papers.  He looked at his watch—12:20.  Perhaps the last ten minutes of Letterman would somehow inspire him to continue.

After listening to a band he'd never heard of, he flipped the station, pausing at every infomercial along the way.  "Using the new Abdomatic for only thirty minutes a day, you'll see dramatic results in only six weeks."  "The Crunch Crusher folds neatly to fit under your bed or store in a closet.  You can even take it along on business trips and vacations."  "Learn to drive the big rigs."  "Now you can instantly and permanently seal anything you want in plastic."  "Earn a degree without ever leaving your home."

Watkins looked over at the stack of papers sitting on his desk. "How about a Gradomatic?" he said out loud as he turned the television off and returned to his desk chair. "How about sealing me in plastic? Why didn't these kids opt for the fun and challenge of driving the big rigs? Why didn't *I* learn to drive the big rigs? Didn't they realize they could have gotten a degree without ever leaving their homes?" He counted the papers again. Still ten, two collated stacks of five essays each, just the way he always stacked them as soon as he received them so that he could work in quotas and finish the labor in a reasonable time. It always gave him the horrible feeling that he was measuring his life out in student essays, but it helped to make the work look manageable. It was a great plan, and had he followed it just once, it would have made his life easier.

At one o'clock in the morning he looked at his watch and calculated the amount of time he'd need to grade the stack. At approximately twenty minutes an essay, he'd be crawling into bed at around 4:30. Deciding to simply forge ahead and see what happened, he picked up the next essay—"My Generation" by Gary Kardell—and read the first line: "In this day of an age, many things can be said about my generation that are not true or are wrong." Watkins looked up from the page, wondering how difficult it could be to maneuver a tractor trailer around city street corners and back it into loading docks. *It couldn't be that hard*, he thought, *and you get to drive all over the country terrorizing people in small cars.*

He returned to the essay and marked a few of the dangling modifiers, the faulty parallel structures, the misspellings, the clichés, and the clumsy expressions. He noted the under-developed paragraphs and the incoherence. He supplied a couple of the missing commas. Even though Watkins often wondered about the impact his comments had on students or their writing, he carefully but succinctly recorded some of his reactions in the margins and wrote a note at the end to alert Gary to the essay's weaknesses, praise his strengths and suggest new approaches. In his final sentence, Watkins encouraged Gary to continue working.

The grade was not hard to figure out; this was not a very good paper, and Watkins knew that it deserved no more than a D+, but he also knew that Gary, a student who struggled valiantly to learn to write and who had shown some slight degree of improvement from the first to the second essay, was going to be very disappointed. This was the part of the job Watkins least enjoyed. Students probably thought that professors loved giving grades, not the process of reading and commenting on essays, but the actual moment of assessment, the opportunity to fail a paper, to drive a stake through the heart of some miserable student. Watkins was sure that students imagined a professor carving a grade into the last page of a paper with a flourish and a sinister laugh, saying "Take that, fool!" Maybe some professors did, but not Watkins. He knew that many students took grades very seriously, often too seriously, and that some took them personally, as if the grade were a reflection of their character. And grading someone's writing was the hardest of all. Many students mistakenly believed that a low grade on their writing meant a low evaluation of their intellectual abilities or a rejection of their beliefs or a discrediting of their deepest feelings. He often wished that he could omit the grade and let the written comment stand alone, but he knew that this would create problems at the end of the semester. He looked in his book at Gary's first two grades— a D and a D+. He slowly and lightly drew a C- on the last page of Gary's essay.

1:20! Watkins was beginning to panic. He could stay up all night working if he had to—he'd done it many times as a student— but he knew that his concentration would waver and that he'd miss too much or become intolerant. He searched through the stack for the paper of someone he could trust to write a good essay, one that wouldn't absorb too much grading time: "Don't Blame Me" by John Zajaczkiewicz:

> People in my age group suffer from a myriad of problems. First, young people today are very anxious about their appearance. They will stand for half an hour before a mirror worrying about their complexion or their hair style or spend their entire week's pay on clothes. They refuse to drive anything other than a Jeep or sporty car. And they will even drastically alter their behavior if they are in the presence of a group of people they want to be accepted by. Second, young people are not very imaginative. Most of them look and dress alike. They act the same way and say the same things. Even though they like to think of

themselves as individuals, they don't act in ways that set them apart from anyone else. These two problems go hand-in-hand. Teenagers worry about their appearance because they don't want to look any different from the rest of society, and wanting to be like everyone else makes them lose their imaginative power. The causes of this problem and the results are also connected.

Our concern with appearances is caused primarily by the media. Television and movies make us think that only good-looking people can be successful. Shows like *Melrose Place* and *Baywatch*, which are popular among teenagers, show how wonderful it is to be beautiful. Ask anyone to name a movie star and they'll say Johnny Depp or Brad Pitt or Jennifer Aniston. It's impossible to name a leading actor or actress who isn't handsome or gorgeous and shapely. And advertisers only use attractive men and women to sell products such as cars and beer. What would happen if a commercial featured a homely person? The ad would probably make fun of the person to sell a product, just in the way David Letterman used to make fun of Larry "Bud" Melman on his show. Another way the media contributes to our concern with appearances is through advertisers pushing the same products all the time. It's getting to the point where a young person feels stupid if he's not wearing the hat or shoes of the week. Ironically, some advertisers sell their products by saying that the customer will be more of an individual by buying the product. How individual can you be when everyone is buying it?

Because we are so concerned with not standing too far out in the crowd, we have lost our power to imagine. Because we dress and talk the same way, we start to think alike, and no one seems to be able to use their creative skills to make themselves into a new and different person. The hardest thing for a young person to do is to take a stand against the group or to disagree with what everyone else is saying. They are afraid of being ostracized and ridiculed. The great irony of all this is that by trying to be the same, young people lose their capacity to appreciate differences and to imagine what it is like to be different. Teenagers become intolerant of anyone who isn't like them, and they start to lose the power to empathize with others who have either decided to be different or who are different by no fault of their own. Members of my generation mock people who are handicapped or smart or black or tall or unathletic or whatever makes them unusual or different. When young people lose the ability to imagine what it's like to be someone else, they have an easier time hurting others.

Unless young people learn to be more willing to go against the crowd and to be their own person, they will never learn to tolerate the differences in others. And we will all end up eventually looking, acting and thinking alike and despising anyone who looks, acts or thinks differently.

*Well*, Watkins thought, *this isn't going to be easy*. He looked at the front of the paper again to remind himself who wrote it. *John Zajaczkiewicz. The quiet kid in the back row. Seems like a nice guy, smart, always wears that cap, good writer*. Watkins read the paper through again, stopping only to mark a few pronoun errors and a touch of wordiness. When he finished reading, Watkins wrote his comment:

John,

Your paper is very interesting. You have obviously given this matter much thought, and your comments prove that you are willing to look deeply at underlying causes for certain behaviors and to look at the possible results of those behaviors. And you provide some interesting and well-chosen support for your comments.

But I think your reader may have some difficulty with the paper's generalities. A reader might get the idea that no one in your generation has any individuality or imagination. There must be some young people who are distinctive and imaginative. There must be some young people who are tolerant of differences and sympathetic toward others. I suspect I can count you as one.

You also might want to clarify the connection between being concerned with appearances and wanting to look like everyone else. I think the problem comes from a confusion between what people desire (individuality) and the result of pursuing that desire (looking and acting alike). Although you hint at that irony, you might want to more fully consider that many young people—many older people, for that matter—*believe* that they are acting as individuals when they chose their manner of dress or speech or behavior. In other words, they are trying, but perhaps their choices are limited. Would that change your approach?

Finally, John, you might want to try to put yourself into your writing. How do you fit into all of this?

Watkins looked at his watch. *My God!* he thought, *ten of!* He'd spent a half an hour on John's paper. He read over his comments, looked at the pencil marks he'd made on John's paper. He tapped the pencil a few times at the bottom of the last page and, finally deciding, scratched a grade beneath his comment.

Watkins managed to get through three more essays before falling into a dead sleep, his forehead resting on the second page of Jen Wiener's five paragraph analysis of the reasons why "kids my age drink so much on the weekend." Specifically, Watkins nodded off at reason number two: "to relieve the pressure of working hard all week." He awoke at around 4:30, went to bed for an additional three-hour dose of anxiety dreams, and arose at 7:00. In his office he finished Jen's essay and two others, but at ten minutes before nine, he decided to return what papers he had finished to their owners and to beg additional time from the other two.

### John

Nervously waiting for Watkins to enter the dark room, John sat listening to the other students talking and joking. Clearly, several friendships had developed in the room since the start of the semester, and the bantering and laughter gave the class an almost festive air, even though some of the students sat shivering from the steady rain they had walked through to get to class. He glanced over at

Eileen, who sat talking animatedly to Tony Falcone, whom John recognized from his dorm, but to whom he'd never spoken.

John's attraction to Eileen had grown stronger, but so had his conviction that someone like her would never have anything to do with someone like him. He had been in love before. Well, to be honest, he had been infatuated with girls before—Mary Ellen Yanoshak in third grade, who promised she'd marry him; Heather Terasavage in seventh grade, who placed first in the district spelling bee when John deliberately misspelled "independent"; Joanne Carlyle in his sophomore year, who threatened to have him decapitated by her boyfriend if he didn't stop looking at her funny; and Caitlin Kitchner, who caused the gash in the side of his head during biology class. He had counted the letters in their names, memorized their phone numbers, carved their initials in various places around his room and on his notebooks, and imagined himself in conversation with them. His only attempt at actual contact after Mary Ellen had been with Heather when he dialed the first six digits of her phone number to congratulate her on winning the spelling bee.

John's reverie was interrupted by Watkins's entrance. "Good morning, everyone," he said, flipping on the lights. John noticed that Watkins looked very tired, but, more important, he noticed that Watkins was carrying a stack of graded essays. Knowing that Watkins had two sections and a large number of papers to grade, John had been prepared for disappointment.

"Before we start today, I need to see two students, Belinda Lindaman and Eileen O'Neill," Watkins announced. John knew that Belinda was out since his foot rested on her chair. He withdrew it instinctively when Watkins looked in the direction of Belinda's desk. He watched Eileen as she walked toward Watkins and as she stood listening to his quiet whispering. John's curiosity was satisfied when Watkins explained his behavior: "I couldn't get all the papers done and I didn't want to hand them back before they were all finished, but Eileen has agreed to wait until later to pick hers up." *A goddess!* John thought. Watkins held the essays as he talked to the class about the need to avoid complacency at mid-semester and about the common errors and problems he was noting in the essays. "Shut up and give us the papers!" John wanted to shout, when he was shocked to hear his thoughts spoken: "You're probably thinking, 'Shut up and give us the papers,' aren't you?" Watkins said. "Okay, here they are, in no particular order. Theodore, Gary, Jennifer, Jennifer? Tony, . . ."

John waited anxiously for his name.

Finally, "John." Watkins was a row away, so John half stood and reached across the row for his essay. Sitting down, he looked at the first page, flipped to the second and studied it, flipped to the third and felt his heart sink. The shock and dismay he felt at seeing a B was compounded by the realization that he'd now have to keep his word to Nick and visit Watkins in his office. He weighed the relative merits of remaining a B-range writer for the rest of his life and looking a professor in the face from only two feet away. Terrified at the thought, he checked his syllabus for Watkins's hours, hoping that they coincided with his classes. "10:30 a.m. to noon, Tuesdays and Thursdays," he read. *Okay, I'll go today. After class. Or Thursday. No, I'll go today. Maybe this afternoon. No, it has to be this morning. Okay, I'll go today. Or Thursday for sure.*

When Watkins dismissed class at 10:15, John remembered all the work he had to do for his afternoon class. He walked back to his room only to find Nick sitting at the desk and Jen sitting on his bed.

"What are you guys doing here?" John asked.

"No class today," Nick said. "Riley's at a conference or something."

"How come you didn't go to class, Jen?"

"It's raining. Hey, did Watkins have our papers?"

John hesitated. The sight of Jen lying on his bed was not unusual. She and Nick often studied in the dorm room to escape her noisy apartment mates. But today she looked especially pretty, her tousled blonde hair giving her the appearance of just having awakened, and the bed appearing all the more cozy and inviting because of the cool air and rain he'd just walked through.

"John!"

"What?"

"Did we get our papers back?" Jen asked slowly.

"Yeah."

"How'd ya do?" Nick asked.

"Good, real good."

"Let's see," Nick responded, snatching the paper out from under John's arm. "Ha! You liar!"

"I thought a B was a good grade, Nick."

"It is, wise-ass, but you said you wouldn't settle for anything less than an A. I'll bet you didn't go to Watkins. I told you you'd chicken out."

"I said I'd go if I got a B+; I got an B. I don't' have to go."

"Oh, great, another lawyer heard from," Nick said.

"Actually, I did go to his office. He's never there."

"Good one. Why don't you go right now? It'll be like going to the dentist. It'll be over before you know it, and it'll do you good."

"Okay, Mom."

"Hey, John," Jennifer asked, "Are your mother and father coming to Parents' Weekend?"

"I don't know yet. I have to ask."

"Well let us know if you're going to the dinner. We'll all get a table together. Leaving the room, John took a few deep breaths and walked slowly back to the Humanities Building and Watkins's office. It was now 10:50. He knocked softly. No answer. As he turned to leave, the door opened.

"I thought I heard a knock. Come in. John, isn't it? What can I do for you, John?"

John walked into Watkins's office and stopped just inside the door. The room was no bigger than a walk-in closet, about eight feet square, covered in a dull yellow paint, with an industrial, gray carpet, a desk and chair, another chair set beside the desk, about twenty books—most of them on the floor—and that was it! Well, there was a wallet-size photograph thumbtacked to the wall just above the desk—but otherwise, nothing! No filing cabinets, bookcases, posters, degrees, desk sets, lamps. John's first thoughts were of a prison cell. There wasn't much room for a bookcase, *But, still*, John thought, *at least decorate the place. What's with this guy?*

"Excuse me, John."

John was startled, thinking Watkins had read his mind, and then realized that he had to move to allow Watkins to close the door. John stepped into the office.

Watkins motioned for John to sit down. "What's up?" he asked.

## *Watkins*

When he returned to his office after class, Watkins pulled a sheet of paper from his desk drawer and began writing:

Dear Diane:

I haven't heard from you in a while, probably because you're keeping your promise to devote every waking moment to your dissertation. I tried to call a few times, but the machine picked up. You must spend all of your time in the library. I hope everything is going well for you. Maybe the discipline will become habitual and  you won't put off grading papers until the last minute the way I do. Of course it took me five years to write the damn dissertation, so it's no surprise that I don't get things done too quickly or at all. You'll be much better at this than I am. In fact, right now I'm suppose to be grading the papers I didn't finish last night.

For the most part my students are bright and friendly. Of course, there are a few I can't stand the sight of. This one guy in my afternoon writing class glares at me for the full period. He checks his watch every minute or so, rolls his eyes, talks to his neighbor, slouches—the entire package. I have nineteen other students in there—all of them good kids—and yet I focus on this one idiot. He misses class now and then, but I never say anything to him about it  because I enjoy class more when he's not there. Maybe after I've taught for twenty more years, I won't care so much about the isolated crazies. But this full paragraph proves that he's on my mind even now. The other students would be upset to know I felt this way, but, on second thought, I'll bet they'd agree with me.

Every graduate school should offer a course in how to teach. Every day I wonder if I'm doing it right. What are they thinking? Do I look like a fool? Am I saying the right things? It's funny that you get to teach at the highest academic level without ever learning how to teach. My only models are people like Bloss and Dreidler and Srakes and some of the other superstars we had at the University. I'm always worried that my students expect me to act like the only models *they* know—the ones from movies and television shows. You know how English professors are always portrayed—giving inspiring lectures filled with quotes they pull from thin air, reaching a powerful crescendo just as the period ends, arousing the women, humbling the men. Yeah. That's me.

And wait till you have a Ph.D. My mother's been bragging about me to her friends. She finds a way to fit "My son, the doctor" into just about every conversation. The other day one of her friends asked what my specialty was. Apparently my mother answered "being a professor," and the friend said "Oh, he's *that* kind of doctor." Well, "she's got another thing comin'" if she thinks my mother will speak to her again. Usually when people find out I have a Ph.D. in English they say "I'd better watch my grammar," or they try to impress me with how smart they are, or they tell me that they could have had a Ph.D., too, but, for some practical reason, they decided not to pursue it. When you get your Ph.D., tell people you drive a truck.

Watkins thought he heard a knock. He quickly wrote "Best, Pete" at the bottom of the page, folded the letter, placed it in his shirt pocket, opened the door and invited John to sit. "What's up?" he asked.

John's answer was to the point: "I'd like to know what I need to do to get an A on an essay."

Watkins could sense John's nervousness and could see that despite the apparent contentiousness in his voice, this student was not mean-spirited or belligerent. Watkins could detect John's tenderness and knew that the roughness of his statement belied his shyness and discomfort. Watkins laughed gently: "Well, John, you might come to see me with your drafts. I could give you some advice before you write the final paper. Why don't you ever come in?"

John just shrugged, so Watkins continued. "From now on, try to come in a few days before the due date, and I'll see if I can help head off some of the problems I see. You know, John, you really are an excellent writer and a bright guy. You shouldn't have any trouble writing at an A level, but you might just need someone to respond to your work before you submit it for a grade. Now let me see your paper."

Watkins took John's essay and read the comment he had written not ten hours earlier. "Okay, John, first, be aware of what's good in your writing: you organize well, your word choices are strong, your sentences are structured nicely, you use good details. But I think I saw in this essay the same problem I saw in the first two: you don't always sound—now don't take this the wrong way—you don't always sound honest."

"You think I'm lying?" John asked, stunned.

"No, you're not being dishonest, John. It just sounds sometimes like you're trying to write the paper you think you *should* be writing, rather than the one you *want* to write. Look at this paragraph. Watkins read aloud the third paragraph of John's essay. "I'm not sure that all young people are as intolerant and cruel as you suggest. I've met a lot of people your age who hang out in very diverse groups and who are broad-minded and generous. True, there's still a great deal of racism and sexism and selfishness, but not *everyone* is like that. I get the feeling, John, that what you're really talking about is the kind of intolerance, prejudice, and cruelty that you've experienced because you feel that you're different from everyone else." John just looked at him in apparent shock. "Am I right, John?"

"Uh, yeah, I suppose."

"Well, why not write about that? Why not write about how it feels to be an outsider, to live outside the group, whether the group has banished you or you've exiled yourself? You could look honestly at some of the reasons that you've been treated the way you have been, and you might even discuss the results of being treated that way. Don't write that everyone your age is intolerant; write that you have been treated with intolerance.

"I can't write about myself, and, besides, the topic was my generation."

"But there are plenty of ways to approach a topic and avoid generalities. And why can't you write about yourself?"

"No one wants to hear about my life."

"But, John, the first exercise you wrote in the class was about you. And it was filled with humor and intelligence. I remember you had a very clever opening and I remember what you wrote about your father." John was silent. "Do you remember that piece?"

"Yeah."

"Well, wasn't it interesting?"

"I suppose. I believe you if you say it was."

"I think anyone would say so, John. You need to realize that you are an interesting person and what you have to say is interesting. Now, I'm not suggesting that everything you write needs to be about you or that you can't write brilliant essays on, say, historical events or that you can't write objective evaluations or reports. In fact, you can write about you generation without using the word "I" anywhere in the essay. But *you* need to work on finding your voice. You know, you've done a wonderful job here of pointing out the cruelty and intolerance you see among young people. Maybe your essay could be an opportunity to ask what you might do about it. Writing can be a means of action, a way of getting involved in your own life. Try something different. Take a risk. And if it doesn't work, and the grade isn't what you'd hoped, well. . . ."

"I know," John interrupted him, "there's more to college than grades."

Watkins laughed. "You remembered. But you still don't believe it."

## John

"I'd like to know what I need to do to get an A on an essay."

*Oh, great, was that aggressive enough? He probably thinks I'm challenging him. Now he'll hate me for sure. Why did I listen to Nick?*

"Why don't you ever come in?" Watkins asked.

*Nick is* so *dead.* John just shrugged. When Watkins suggested that John's writing was dishonest, John could feel himself blush. *Does he know something? He couldn't.* But the comment was shocking enough to send his mind reeling while Watkins offered suggestions for improving his writing. John composed himself enough to hear most of what Watkins said, and when Watkins asked "Am I right?" he knew to say yes. When Watkins recommended writing personally, John was incredulous. Then Watkins mentioned that first exercise. Good, he didn't suspect anything. *Okay*, he thought, *I'll find my voice, even though I'm not really sure what that means. I'll try something different. I'll take a risk.*

When the conference ended, John stood up. "Thanks, Professor Watkins. I'm sorry I bothered you."

"You're joking! You didn't bother me. I enjoyed talking to you, and besides, this is what they pay me for."

Just then someone knocked on the door. "Come in," Watkins said. As John turned around in the six square-feet of space between the chair and the door, the door opened, and Eileen O'Neill stepped into the exact same six square-feet. For a fraction of a moment, John looked directly into her eyes. He gasped uncontrollably and instinctively looked at the floor. And then he danced with Eileen O'Neill. He moved to his left; she moved to her right. He moved right; she moved left. Right, left. Left, right. He started making what he would later convince himself were screaming noises but were really only soft "ums" and "uhs" as he desperately tried to figure out where to go. Then for some reason, he sat back down in the chair next to Watkins's desk and studied the gray carpet. *Of all the offices in the world*, he thought.

"I'm sorry to bother you, Professor. . ." *Oh, it's no bother; this is what they pay him for*, John thought and then panicked believing that he had spoken out loud. He could feel the sweat under his cap. "I just came by to get my paper."

"I'm sorry, Eileen, I didn't get a chance to grade it yet," Watkins answered.

*Oh, right, it's my fault,* John thought, imagining that Watkins was nodding slyly toward him and trying to sense whether or not Eileen was looking at him. *Nick is deader than dead.*

"Can you come back in about half an hour?"

"Sure," Eileen said, convincing John even more that she truly was the nicest, kindest, classiest, most thoughtful, understanding, compassionate, humane, and best looking woman on campus.


### Eileen

Having nervously gulped a cup of coffee, certain that Watkins had deliberately failed to return her paper so that he'd have a reason to call her to the office and discuss the missing essay number two, Eileen returned to Watkins's office, knocked and entered at his invitation. "I hope I'm not too soon," she said apologetically. Watkins assured her that she wasn't, and motioned for her to sit.

"Your essay is remarkable," Watkins began. I don't think I've ever had a student who writes with so much honesty and passion. Your words seem to come straight from the heart. I can't imagine that it is easy to write about these things. I loved what you said about the love and support you found among your high school friends. Your comments on how a person's good side can be repressed or drawn out are excellent. I especially like the details. That one friend of yours—what was her name, Kristina?—she sounds like a trip."

"Yeah, she really is." Eileen thought Watkins was giving her a lot of credit; she hadn't even used the word *repressed*. "I enjoyed writing it in a way," Eileen responded. "It helps me to express what I'm feeling. I guess it's like therapy." She felt the need to apologize quickly. "I couldn't write the second paper you assigned, though. I tried so many times, but I couldn't say what I wanted to and everything I did say sounded stupid."

Eileen couldn't tell if Watkins was pretending not to remember her topic, but when he asked to be reminded of it, she answered,

66

"my family. I had no trouble writing the first essay about myself, and the third I could handle—about my generation. But writing about my family was too difficult. There's so much sadness I felt morbid writing about them. I just couldn't do it. You probably think I'm just making excuses for not handing in a paper."

"I believe you," Watkins said, though Eileen was not persuaded. She realized that people who knew her situation often treated her delicately, and she sometimes suspected their motives. Did he really believe her, or was she benefiting from Watkins's apparently sympathetic nature? She decided not to pursue the matter. Watkins spent the next fifteen minutes discussing Eileen's family and helping her find a more manageable topic and approach. In the end, they decided that she would complete the assignment with an illustrative essay on her little sister's personality. "I don't have anything this afternoon," Eileen said. "I'll write a draft and bring it to you tomorrow."

"Sounds great," Watkins said. But don't feel that you have to get it to me so quickly. Tuesday will be fine."

Eileen got up to leave. "Thanks, Professor. I'll see you next week. Enjoy the weekend."

"Wait," Watkins said. "Don't you want your other essay?"

"Oh, yeah, I forgot that's why I came in." She took the essay from Watkins, thanked him and left the office. In the hall, she looked at her grade, a B, and at Watkins's comment, where he repeated what he'd already mentioned in the office and suggested ways to improve the essay's organization, development and paragraph structure. She looked at the scattered corrections in her text. Happy with her work, Eileen folded the paper and tucked it into the back pocket of her jeans. Leaving the building, she anxiously looked to see if school's weekly paper, *The Read and White*, had been delivered yet.


### Watkins

When Eileen left his office, Watkins unfolded his letter to Diane and read with disgust the words he had written. Despite knowing that it said nothing he wanted to say, he sealed the letter in a envelope, which he addressed, stamped, and carried to the campus post office. He spent the remainder of the day in his normal routine, having lunch alone in his office and teaching his afternoon class. At 3:30 he left the building, stopping at the front door to pick up a copy of the school paper. In the light rain still falling, he jogged to his car without looking at the paper, until he settled into his car and was struck by the headline. He read the entire piece.

# Student Accused of Racism
## Campus Divided on Issue

College officials again yesterday defended their decision to charge Anthony Falcone with harassment and hate speech for his behavior during a party this past weekend at the Doral Apartments, a residence building owned by Wexford College. Falcone is accused of provoking a fight with James Washington and shouting racist epithets at him.

"We've been investigating this situation for the past few days and have decided that the charges are warranted," Dean Matthews said yesterday. "We have spoken to at least half a dozen people who were at the party, and almost all of them have given the same description of what they saw and heard." According to witnesses, Falcone apparently confronted Washington in one of the apartment's bedrooms, pushed him and shouted "You

don't even deserve to be here, you stupid gorilla." The two men scuffled before others at the party broke them apart. According to the charges against Falcone, he shouted, "You people want it all," as some of his friends dragged him from the apartment.

Falcone has denied some of the charges. In an interview with the college paper, he agreed that he may have pushed Washington, but challenged the other charge. "There's no way I said anything racial to him," Falcone insists. "I'm not a racist, and I would never say something like that."

When asked about witnesses who heard him call Washington a "gorilla," Falcone insisted that he was referring to Washington's strength and size. Washington, a wide-receiver on the college football

68

team, is over six-feet tall and weighs about 220 pounds. Falcone also plays for the Cardinals. Falcone further insists that by "you people," he meant simply "guys like Washington, but not black guys, just guys like him."

Witnesses at the party told college investigators and administrators that the fight apparently resulted from the fact that both Washington and Falcone competed for the same position on the college's football team, a position that both men have shared in the first four games.

Several partygoers interviewed for this story claimed that the scuffle between the two was not violent or all that serious. "These two guys are teammates," said Jonathan Silkes. "They were just fooling around. This is a team thing. Everyone is blowing this way out of proportion. Tony didn't do anything so awful."

Several students agreed with Silkes. A sophomore, who asked not to be identified, said that the school is overreacting. "No one got hurt," she said. "The school should just let these two students settle the issue between them." According to another student, a senior, "You can't say anything anymore, even at a party, without someone charging you with harassment or something."

Other students are certain that a serious crime was committed. Adam Hengerst, a sophomore, is angry about the incident. "We shouldn't tolerate this sort of thing here," he said. "There's enough racism in the world. I think Falcone should be expelled."

Washington himself could not be reached for comment, although several friends of Washington's told the paper that he was not upset. Accusations are coming mostly from observers, they said.

One student is withholding judgment. "I wasn't there," said Eileen O'Neill, a first-year student; "I'm not sure what happened. I know Tony Falcone and he seems like a sweet guy. I guess we'll just have to wait and see."

The campus will have to wait until October 29, the scheduled date for Falcone's disciplinary hearing.

Watkins was stunned—first at his obliviousness; he had just seen Eileen, and both she and Tony had attended the morning class, and second at the possibility that something like this could occur at Wexford. People of color made up only a small percentage of the student body—in fact, as far as he could tell by appearance or name, Jessica was the only non-white student in his morning writing class—but for the most part they seemed in Watkins's limited view to enjoy the college, and in his few months at Wexford, Watkins had seen nothing that he would call "racist," although he realized that he had little contact with the students outside of class.


### John

"What do you think of this, John? I'm not surprised, of course. People around here are acting so shocked. What'd they think, that we're immune from this kind of bullshit behavior. You know this guy Falcone lives in this building? I'll kill him when I see him. I'll tell you sometimes this place really gets to me."

"What are you talking about, Nick?" John asked.

"This! This!" Nick forcefully stabbed his finger at the newspaper article.

"Let me see," John said taking the paper and reading the first paragraph.

"Tony Falcone! He's Eileen's boyfriend. I mean he's in my class. I know him! Well, sort of. I really don't know him very well except that he's in my writing class. Do you know this guy Washington?"

"Yeah, real good. He's a great guy. I'm sure he could have crushed this little puke, but he's not the type to get into brawls."

John continued to read. At the end of the article he jumped off the bed. "She's defending him! I can't believe this! 'A sweet guy!' What's that supposed to mean? Oh, this is too much. This really sucks. Defending a racist! This doesn't sound like her. Maybe it's a misquote. Maybe they quoted her out of context. Maybe she said 'sweaty guy' and they misunderstood."

"Now it's my turn to ask what the hell you're talking about, John."

"Eileen O'Neill is defending Tony Falcone."

"Well, I'm glad to see you've sorted out the important issues here." He snatched the paper from John's hands.

"I'm sorry, Nick. You're right. This is a lousy way to treat someone. I'm sorry."

"Well don't apologize to me," Nick responded. "It's Washington who was mistreated here. I'm going to be very interested in seeing how the school handles this."

# Tuesday, October 21

### John

John hadn't been sure if by "the school" Nick meant the administration or the students, but during the weekend that followed the article's appearance in the paper, he discovered that administrators were more united in their condemnation of the act than the students were. Students supported Tony, cursed him, justified his actions, denounced him, sympathized with his feelings, wished to see him expelled. Some dismissed the entire matter as Jonathan Silkes had—an insignificant incident blown out of proportion and distorted by emotion. But for many others, this apparently meaningless incident suggested deep-seated, attitudes among the student body toward race and racial differences.

"It's easy to say 'insignificant' if it's not you that's involved!" Jen Wiener announced angrily to those gathered in her writing class on Tuesday morning at five minutes before nine. "If you were black and someone called you a 'gorilla,' you might feel different. You might be hurt by that."

Jen made no effort to hide her feelings, and because Tony Falcone had not yet come in, no one else had to worry about what was said. The conversation moved quickly, and John listened intently without tossing his opinion into the fray.

"I think 'gorilla' could mean a number of things. Maybe Tony was being honest when he said that he was referring to Washington's size."

"That's interesting. You call Tony Falcone by his first name and James Washington by his last name."

"So what? Is that evidence of my racism? I know Tony because he's in this class, that's all."

Another student got involved: "Man, it's true! See, you can't say anything these days. First name, last name. Who cares? Every time you open your mouth you're offending someone. You couldn't even talk about the baseball playoffs without upsetting some Indian tribes."

"Listen to your tone. You say the words 'Indian tribes' as if you were spitting out an insect that flew into your mouth." It was Jessica. John could clearly see that she was speaking from experience. "I constantly feel insulted—not so much by *what* people say, but *how* they say it. I don't mind when people say that Asian students are good at math. I mind when they say it as if they hate us for it."

The door opened, abruptly halting the conversation as everyone looked to see who was entering. "What?" asked Matthew Martin, surprised to see everyone looking at him. "What'd I do?"

"What do you think about the Falcone incident?" someone asked him.

"Who cares?" he responded flippantly.

"I care," Jen almost shouted. "I care, and so should you, and so should everyone in this room and in this school. These are real people who are getting hurt by our behavior." She turned to look directly at John, and he could read in her wide eyes and tight jaw a plea for help. "Say something," she was begging silently. Fearful of the sound of his own voice in an occupied room, he just shrugged. Jen, obviously on the verge of tears, clumsily gathered her things and walked quickly out of the room.

"What's her problem?" someone asked.

"I'm not sure, but I don't like how she said 'our behavior,'" Ann Marie Albright offered. "I don't see how Tony Falcone's behavior is my behavior. I don't act that way toward minorities, and I'm certainly not a racist."

"I think you can believe you're not a racist and still do things that are racist or have thoughts that are racist. Be honest, if you see a black man walking toward you on an isolated street, aren't you just the slightest bit nervous?" The question came from Pete Churnip.

"No, absolutely not!" Ann Marie insisted. "In fact, I might even smile at him and say, "Hi."

"Why?"

"To let him know that I'm not afraid of him and that I'm not worried about his being African-American."

"But don't you see that there's a touch of racism even in that?"

"Oh," she responded sarcastically, "so by being nice, I'm being racist."

"In a way, yes. I think the issue is very complicated. It's probably best to just say that if you're white, you probably have a touch of racism in you. It can't be helped."

"So what nice things do you do that are racist?" Ann Marie asked defensively.

"Well," Pete answered immediately, "if I see a photograph of a bunch of real successful business leaders, and one or a few of them are black, I almost instinctively think, hey, a black guy made it. I'm happy for him, but I'd like to get to the point where I didn't even notice his color, because even noticing is just a bit racist." He indicated how much with his fingers.

"I think, hey, affirmative action!" someone said apparently trying to be comical but failing. Pete tsked loudly.

The door opened. "I am so sorry I'm late," Watkins said. John looked at the clock. It was ten after nine. "I'm glad to see you waited." John and the rest of the class just looked at the intruder. "I was on. . . ." He paused. "What's going on? Did I miss something?"

"Yeah," Pete Churnip said with disgust. "Billy Bob here thinks successful African-Americans got where they are because someone gave them a free ride."

Billy Bob—really Robert Henderson, who John recognized because he lived on Johns' floor—responded quickly and roughly: "Shut up, Pete."

"Good argument, Bob, you win."

"Wait a minute," Watkins insisted. "What's going on? Why all the angry looks? Ann Marie, what's up?"

"We were talking about the incident last week with Tony." Almost everyone in the class, including John, turned automatically to look at Tony's desk as if to assure themselves that he had not sneaked into the room and overheard the conversation.

"Tony's not coming to class," Watkins said. "He called me this morning to say that he'd be out for the week. I don't want to stop your discussion. It's probably a good idea to get some of your thoughts and feelings out."

No one responded. The discussion had flown freely without a judge or referee, and no one seemed willing to start it up again. After a few moments of uncomfortable silence, someone said, "I don't think we should take a stand on Tony's guilt or innocence until we know more about the incident." John's heart sank. It was Eileen O'Neill, who until now had been as silent as he.

"Go on, Eileen," Watkins said.

"I really don't have much more to say," she replied. "I don't know Tony very well, and I'm not sure if anyone in here does. How do we know that he even said what he's accused of saying or that he is a racist?"

*She doesn't know him very well!* John thought. *This is good news.* Then he remembered Nick's admonition and Jen's desperate look and felt sick with guilt. He vowed to stop thinking about Eileen's relationship with Tony and to concentrate on the debate.

Belinda Lindaman anted up: "There were witnesses. Even his girlfriend said that what was in the newspaper was, you know, exactly what he said. She was there. She heard him."

His girlfriend! John's thoughts were so loud and spontaneous that they were as close as thoughts can come to being spoken out loud. *He has a girlfriend. Eileen would never settle for that. Maybe she's single.* He remembered his pledge. *Shit! Okay, forget her for a while. Ponder this wonderful news later.*

"Yeah," someone said. "There were witnesses."

"Okay," Eileen said, "what if he did say 'gorilla'? We can't know what was in his heart. We don't know what he intended. We don't know who he truly is."

Watkins interrupted. "Why don't we sort out the issues and approach this more methodically? As I see it there are several main questions. He wrote them on the board. Did Tony say what he is accused of saying? If he did say what he said, can we call him a racist? And even if he is a racist, should he be allowed to say what he said? Let's start with the first one—did Tony say what he is accused of saying? Can you prove it?"

"I think the answer is easy, Professor," Matthew said, pulling the newspaper from his book bag. "Here it is: 'You don't even deserve to be here, you stupid gorilla,' and 'You people want it all.' There it is in black and white."

"Well don't believe everything you read in the paper, Matthew," Eileen warned him.

"But there were witnesses," Belinda said, exasperated. "No one is listening to me."

"She's right," someone said. "Half a dozen. Six people. Did six people all hear the same wrong thing? I mean, I doubt it."

"Well," Eileen fired back, but patiently and beautifully, "how do we know what the interview was like? Maybe the reporter asked someone at a table and the other five kids at the table all said, 'Oh, yeah, that's what he said.' Besides, it says in the paper 'almost all' of the witnesses gave the same account. And that's what a reporter is saying Dean Matthews said. You can never be sure about things."

"Were you on O.J.'s defense team?" Theodore Crossings asked. Everyone laughed.

"That's actually a good point," Watkins said. "The difference between what happened and what people remember happening and how the evidence can be interpreted and passed along—well, you can get lost in all the complications. Let's just say that we have six people who claim to have all heard the same thing. What other evidence might you try to gather to determine if Tony said what he supposedly said?"

"I would ask him," Belinda said. "In fact, didn't the reporter ask him?"

"Oh, yeah," several students said at once.

"Duh," Matthew said, mocking himself and the rest of the class. "It's right here: 'When asked about witnesses who heard him call Washington a "gorilla," Falcone insisted that he was referring to Washington's strength and size. Washington, a linebacker on the college football team, is over six-feet tall and weighs about 250 pounds. Falcone also plays for the Cardinals. Falcone further insists that by "you people," he meant simply "guys like Washington, but not black guys, just guys like him."' I would take that as evidence that Tony said it."

"I would too," Watkins said. "Tony doesn't seem to be denying that he said 'gorilla' and 'you people.' Now, are those racist terms? And, perhaps more important, do they indicate that Tony is racist?"

"Is there a difference?" someone asked.

"I think so," Watkins said. "I think you have to consider the context. I could certainly use the word 'gorilla' without being racist, if I'm at the zoo, for an obvious example. Or what if I call my large white friend a gorilla? I could say I was referring to his size and no one could accuse me of racism. Now, if I say the same thing to my large black friend, couldn't I say that I'm not a racist, I just wasn't thinking of how it might sound when I said it? I certainly wouldn't intend it to be racist."

"I think that's different, Professor," Jessica said. "You're right that context matters for a word like this, but if you use a word like *gorilla* in this context, can't you say that it's a racist term whether you intended it or not? I remember a few years ago when a sports broadcaster got all excited seeing a football player, who happened to be black, run the ball down field and the announcer said 'Look at that monkey run!' If the runner had been white, nothing would have happened, but he was black, so the announcer got in all sorts of trouble. You need to be very careful with words. I think that in the case of your black friend, you have to be sensitive enough to consider how he might react and chose a different word to indicate his size. Would you be more sensitive to your white friend?"

"Good question," Watkins responded. "I think you're right to suggest that being insensitive to others who are different is a form of racism. Thank you for reminding me of that. It occurs to me that we could define racism to include a lack of empathy. Okay, how about if we word the question this way: "Even though Tony made an insensitive and racist remark, can we say that it was a *momentary* lapse in sensitivity and that it does not indicate that he has a racist *nature*?"

"I think that's fair, although maybe we shouldn't call anyone a gorilla" said Eileen. "We should be able to forgive one another for isolated cases of insensitivity. Shouldn't we try to find out if this is how Tony usually acts, or whether it is an isolated incident? I haven't seen any evidence—any other evidence, I guess I should say—that Tony is racist. He seems like a. . . ." She paused.

"A sweet guy?" Watkins asked with a grin.

Everyone, including John, laughed, not derisively, and turned to look at Eileen, who blushed slightly, smiled and said, "Yeah, a sweet guy."

Students were still chuckling and one was falling further in love with Eileen, when a student who'd been quiet to this point said something to silence the class. "Okay, maybe he was just saying that Washington's big, but he was right when he said they're taking everything." In the several seconds of perfect silence that followed, students looked alternatively at Watkins and the commentator as if watching them exchange an invisible tennis ball.

"I'm sorry," Watkins eventually said, as if giving the student a few more seconds to change his thinking. "What did you say, Chris?"

"I said that Tony is right about them wanting everything. They've got the jobs, the good schools, the sports. Nothing is safe anymore. They even have golf now."

"Who's they?" Watkins asked.

"You know who," Chris answered—stressing "you" as if to say "Don't play dumb,"—"the minorities." The way he said "minorities"—in a sarcastic whine that some parents use to mock their children—clearly angered Watkins, who, gasping and stammering slightly, quickly cut Chris off.

"Huh, please, Chris, please, uh, try to keep to the issues!" Surprised by Watkins's abruptness, John was equally astonished by his control. Judging from the look on his face, John expected Watkins to explode, and he wondered why a professor so detached from the situation would care so much about a student's attitude. Watkins's restraint was remarkable, John thought; he even invited Chris to continue. "Would you like to develop your point?" Watkins asked.

"No, thank you," Chris replied flatly.

"Well, I would," Bob said. "I know what Chris means. It's gettin' to where you feel like if you're white you don't belong anymore. You can't say or do anything. You know, Pete says everybody's a racist. Well, I think everybody who isn't white expects to be treated with racism. If you say to a black guy, 'You should study harder,' he'll say, 'Oh, are you saying blacks don't study hard?' You get accused of racism even though you didn't mean nothing by the comment. I think Washington overreacted. Besides, he probably is a gorilla."

A number of students groaned loudly. Some grunted angrily.

But having an ally apparently increased Chris's courage. "Women are the same way," he said. "A few weeks ago I held a door open for a woman, and she said, 'Excuse me, I can hold my own door, thank you. Don't be such a pig.' Can you believe it?"

"What did you say?" Pete Churnip asked.

"I said, 'Gee, Mom, I was only trying to help.'"

Everyone laughed.

"I didn't say a word," Chris continued. She just wanted someone to yell at. She was one of them feminazis. She just wanted to be in charge of me."

"I'll assume you're still joking," Pete said, turning to look at Chris. But seriously, you could have just said that you would hold the door for anyone. Wouldn't you?"

"You mean for a guy? Not likely."

"Then you *are* a sexist, a chauvinist."

There was some upheaval in the class. "Pete," Ann Marie said, "You don't give anyone a break. I like when guys hold the door for me," she said in an exaggeratedly flirtatious tone, batting her eyelashes at Chris.

A few moments more of silence followed, until Watkins asked, "Well, what about Tony's comment, 'you people want it all'?" Is that a racist comment? Does anyone want to speculate on what Tony may have meant by that?

"I think it's the same issue as the gorilla comment," Belinda said. "He might have simply meant, you know, guys like him. I mean, you know, big guys. I agree with Eileen. I think it would be, you know, best to find out what kind of guy Tony is. If he does stuff like this all the time, I think we could, like, call him a racist. I mean a *real* racist, not the kind that everybody is, according to Pete."

"You know," someone said, "I'm starting to wonder if we should define that word. What exactly is a *racist*? What constitutes *racism*?"

"Great questions, Mike," Watkins said. "What is racism?"

The conversation carried over for several minutes after the end of the period. Finally Watkins said, "I guess we should go. I didn't get to anything I had planned for today, but that's okay. In fact, let's continue our conversation during Thursday's class. I'd like to ask you a few more questions. First, are there any other possible explanations for what Tony said? And even if you conclude that Tony's comments *were* racially motivated, and even if he *is* a racist by our definition, do you think the school should be able to charge him with harassment and hate speech, as Dean Matthews has suggested?"

As the students walked from the class, John could hear that few of them were content to wait until Thursday to settle the debate. And out of the corner of his eye, he could see Eileen handing something to Watkins.

### Watkins

Earlier that same morning, Watkins had sat in his office looking over his notes for his upcoming class. For only the second or third time all semester, Watkins truly *felt* prepared for class. He was almost always prepared, but today he was armed with more ideas, notes, exercises, illustrations, examples, and handouts than ever before. When you're prepared for class, twenty minutes is a lifetime, he reasoned, and, putting his notes aside, took a sheet of paper from his desk drawer "Dear Diane," he began. He was thinking of an opening line when the phone rang.

"Professor Watkins?"

"Yes."

"Hi, it's Tony Falcone. I'm in your writing class."

"Yes, Tony."

"I'm not going to be able to make it into class today. I have to meet with Dean Matthews and some other people to prepare for my disciplinary hearing."

"Did you tell the Dean you had class at 9:00?"

"Well," Tony said hesitating, "actually, the meeting is at 10:00, but I, uh, I . . . "

"You don't want to come to class," Watkins said to finish Tony's sentence.

"Yes. People haven't been very friendly toward me, so I think I'll just wait until this whole thing is over."

"It might not be over for a while."

"Well, maybe for another few classes, just to give things a chance to cool down."

Watkins invited Tony to come to the office to keep up with the work, and Tony agreed to visit.

"Tony, before you hang up I should tell you that the situation might come up in class today."

"That's okay, Professor. I don't mind if you talk about it."

"All right, Tony. Can I ask you a question, if you don't mind?"

"You want to know if I did it."

"You don't have to say anything, Tony. Maybe it's none of my business."

"I don't mind telling you. I did say what they said I said, and I did push Jim. But I wasn't being a racist. It's kinda stupid. We have this thing on the team where in practice we call each other, you know, animal names if we do something like an animal. If someone runs the ball back real fast, he's the 'Cheetah' for that day or if a linebacker slices up the middle, he's the 'Tiger.' If some big guy does something stupid like drill his own guy in the back, he's the 'Gorilla.' Jim knows that's what I meant. And when I said, you know, guys like him, I only meant the starters. They think they can play any position forever. I compete with Jim for the same spot, but we get along. The whole team does. There's no racism in those guys. I just lost my cool."

"I appreciate your explanation, Tony. I hope everything works out for you. Although you might have to find a new animal for the dumb guys. You're not being fair to gorillas, you know. They're pretty smart."

"Don't worry," Tony replied. "The guys have already started calling dumb players the "Falcone.""

Watkins laughed, wished Tony good luck, set the receiver down and thought about his explanation. Was it just another ingenious defense? Was it just the clever reasoning of a creative student, or did the football team, like so many groups of people, invent a custom that might appear silly to outsiders? Watkins checked his watch. "Holy shit!" he said out loud, grabbed his books and bolted from the office.

*    *    *

10:15. Returning to his office after class, Watkins noticed the blank letter to Diane still sitting on his desk. He sat down, picked up a pen and wrote, "I love this job. When you become a teacher, brag about it to anyone who will listen. I just had the best class of my career. I know it's a short career so far, but I can't imagine it gets any better than this." He set the pen and his stack of materials on the desk. Noticing Eileen's essay on top, he started to read:

Essay #2
My Sister
My sister blames herself for our mother's death because Maury, my sister, waited until the last minute to tell my mother that she needed a soccer T-shirt for the mini team she played on. So my mother was driving at around 9:00 on a Friday night trying to get to the store before they closed and she was hit broadside by a drunk driver. Maury was hurt pretty bad, but she survived, and to this day she has no physical scars only mental ones. She is very afraid to do anything without permission and she apologizes all the time. But she wasn't always like this. Under the sadness there is one of the smartest, funniest and kindest people I know.

When she was only five years old Maury went around the house and collected up every pen and pencil she could find and hid them somewhere. It wasn't many because we didn't have a lot, but she hid them all. Then when someone in the house was desparate searching for a pen or pencil to write down a phone number or make a grocery list, Maury would offer to sell them one. My father would be on the phone saying "just a minute, I'm looking for a pen" and this little girl would be holding one out saying "for only a dollar you can have this one." If my father went to grab it she ran, usually he bought the pen. Or he would just tell the person on the phone to go ahead and he would memorize, or I should say try to memorize the number. He never got mad at her because she was so cute about it. But he did get just a little upset when it was raining one day and he couldn't find an umbrella anywhere and Maury had this huge grin on her face.

I also remember one incident that shows how funny she can be. We were in a store like a K-mart. Maury was only about four years old. My mother was helping me pick out some clothes and we weren't paying a lot of attention to Maury. Don't get the idea we weren't keeping an eye on her, but we didn't see her find a sticker and stick it to her shirt. The sticker said Hi, my name is Pete. It must have been one of the worker's nametags. Maury didn't even know what it said, so I told her and for the next week or so she wore that nametag and insisted on being called Pete. She would stick out her hand to perfect strangers and say "Hi, my name is Pete. What's yours?" Every now and then we still call her Pete.

A final part of my sister's personality can be shown in what she did about a mouse that my father caught. My father is a very sweet man, but he is macho in an old fashioned way. One time he caught a mouse on that sticky paper that traps their feet. He took the mouse which was still alive and wrapped it in newspaper and smacked it with his hammer to kill it. My sister went nuts, she screamed at him that she would run away if he ever did that again. So another time when he caught a mouse with the same kind of paper, he said "Maury, what do you suggest we do about this". She took the mouse on the paper and used scissors to cut the paper around the mouses feet so that it looked like the mouse was wearing little snow shoes. Then she took it outside and set it free to run into the woods wearing those little flat yellow shoes. I remember my mother laughing and crying at the same time when she saw that.

I hope that someday Maury can go back to what she was before the accident. I love her with all my heart and I would do anything for her. But sometimes I miss Pete.

All of his breath left Watkins at once. He picked up his pen, and on the letter to Diane he wrote, "It just got better."

"Come in," he said, responding to a knock at his door. It was Gary Kardell.

"Professor Watkins, I'm in your morning class. I'm sorry I missed today. I've been sick," a point he attempted to prove with a detailed account of the evening's various bodily discharges.

"It's okay, Gary. It's okay," Watkins interrupted in a cheerful voice.

"Well," Gary returned, "I was just wondering if we did anything important today."

# CHAPTER III

# Thursday, October 23

Watkins opened the door to room 312 on Thursday morning at 9:00 to find the room buzzing with conversation. Thrilled to find his students excited about continuing the discussion suspended at the end of Tuesday's class, he eavesdropped while pretending to study the roster.

"It took me all week to clean the room. I had to make sure I removed all traces of my boyfriend's existence. They'd kill me."

"I think they got the last room at the Hilton. My father couldn't believe the cost."

"I can't wait to see them. I miss them so much."

"Hey, does anyone know the Sunday Mass schedule at the church on Jefferson Street?"

"Are you going to the dinner-dance?"

"Who are we playing that weekend?"

"I hope the game's good. My mother loves football games—not watching them on TV, but going to them."

*Parents' Weekend!* He could hear the various tones of excitement, anxiety, anticipation and nervousness. At first he was disappointed that they had apparently forgotten Tony Falcone and Jim Washington, but he was not surprised at the natural ebb and flow of interest that young people—no, all people—show toward serious events, and he found endearing their excitement and just the fact that they were discussing their parents.

"I see you're all preparing to show your parents that they're getting their money's worth, huh?" he asked the class. "Well, I hope it's a good weekend for you. Let's have a short class today, and you can get on with the chore of cleaning your rooms and drilling your friends on what can and cannot be mentioned in front of your parents." They laughed. "Okay, where were we? We decided that Tony's apparent insensitivity could qualify him as a racist if we define that term to mean, among other things, that we fail to show the same sensitivity toward one group that we normally show toward another. So beyond actively oppressing a group of people, racists also refuse, perhaps unwittingly, to show that group the same courtesies he or she shows other groups. Does that sound like an accurate summary?"

Silence. A few slow nods.

"Have I misrepresented the consensus?" Watkins asked. "Eileen, is that a fair representation of what we discussed?"

"It sounded like it. Yes."

"How about the rest of you?"

More silence. A few sighs. Watkins began to sense the class's boredom. He had been holding a manila folder, which he tossed in an exaggerated show of disgust on the desk. "You people are amazing," he said. "You have to be the most apathetic, laziest, stupidest people I've ever known. Just plain dumb." His voice was filled with contempt and derision. Several of the students looked genuinely surprised, several looked hurt, one looked angry. Watkins continued: "In the years since I started teaching in graduate school, I can't remember meeting a larger bunch of imbeciles, fools, dunderheads, dunces, dolts"—his mental thesaurus was wide open—"morons, half-wits, dimwits, simpletons, imbeciles . . . ."

"You said 'imbeciles,'" Ann Marie interrupted.

Watkins smiled. He could see that some of the students were catching on, but clearly some were not.

"I don't get it. What's funny now?" Matthew Martin asked. "You attack us and smile. I don't understand."

"I attacked you? I didn't touch you," Watkins responded.

Theodore Crossings spoke up: "Well, you're abusing us by calling us names."

Several more students were apparently catching on. "You're harassing us, right? Just like, you know, Tony harassed Jim Washington," Belinda said.

"Well, that's the question, isn't it?" Watkins answered. He waited for a reaction, but none was forthcoming. The same silence that greeted him earlier fell on the class.

"Hello. Is there anybody out there?" Watkins said gently.

"I think people are sick of talking about it," Theodore explained.

"That's understandable," Watkins returned. "You can start to feel fatigued or even bored after talking for too long about controversial issues."

"Except if they involve you directly," Jen Wiener exclaimed.

"That's very true," Watkins responded. Let's hold off for a few minutes on the incidents that took place on campus last week and talk about what happened here in the classroom this morning. Some of you realized after a while that I was making a point, but before you realized that, how did you *feel*?"

No one responded, so Watkins, who seldom called on students who hadn't volunteered to speak, suddenly felt comfortable or brave enough to select a student to respond to his question. He chose Matthew, who had found nothing funny in the attack. "Matthew, you weren't too happy when I was calling you all names. Why not?"

"I knew you were trying to make a point," Matthew replied curtly.

*Great choice*, Watkins thought. *The one time I call on someone, he's defensive.* He knew he had to handle this situation delicately or risk appearing to actually harass a student. "I know you realized that, but at first were you even slightly upset with me?"

"Maybe just a little, but not really."

"I was pissed," Watkins heard from the right side of the room, followed by a few giggles from elsewhere. He turned.

"Who was pissed?"

"Me."

"Why, Theodore? What did I do to anger you?"

"Calling us names," he responded incredulously. "'Stupid jerks' and all that."

"Did I say 'stupid jerks'?"

"I don't know," Theodore said, his voice rising. "You said a lot of things."

Watkins could see that the student was still agitated. "You're still upset by this, aren't you, Theodore?"

"Yeah, I am. I don't think it's fair for a teacher to come into a classroom and start yelling at his students."

Now Watkins was getting defensive. "I didn't yell, I don't think."

"I don't mean yell like you screamed or nothing. I mean yelled at us like made us feel like kids."

Watkins could see that this issue was becoming very complicated and that the course of the conversation was turning from his intended purpose to a debate on whether his methods were effective. *Oh my God*, he thought. *They want to talk about how I teach.* He knew he was in dangerous waters. "Okay," he said, trying to give himself time to think, "okay, okay now, all right. I think there are two issues here, but they're related. There's the issue of a person saying things that are intended to upset another person, and there's the issue of my trying to goad you all into a conversation by calling you names. I hope you see that I wasn't really calling you names; I was just trying to make a point. I was trying to get you to see what it's like to be verbally abused."

"Okay, how about if we start verbally abusing you?" Theodore asked.

Watkins could feel beads of sweat rolling down his sides. He immediately thought of all the possible names students could invent for a slightly pudgy, longhaired, stressed-out, unmarried young English professor. "Please don't," he asked with a slight laugh in his voice, a laugh he was grateful to hear echoed by several other students. But Theodore would not relent.

"Why not?"

Watkins quickly looked around the room. If there *were* a manual for teaching college, this predicament would not be in it. Not only was the class taking this in a direction he had not anticipated; the focus was on him. Seeing the curiosity and the apprehension on the faces of the other students, he thought for a moment that he'd rather be anywhere else. He would have welcomed assistance, but someone coming to his aid risked appearing obsequious. He was on his own. "Well," he finally said, "you'd embarrass me."

"Ha, you embarrassed us!"

"Did I? I didn't single you out. I was attacking the entire class. I mean attacking to make a point, of course. But I didn't pick on anyone in particular." He saw some light. "By abusing the entire class—to make a point," he added raising his eyebrows and his index finger, "I could be accused of other faults but not embarrassing you individually. Maybe if I had believed that you were imbeciles I could be accused of stereotyping or of assuming that your silence meant you were dumb. But I didn't embarrass anyone in particular. Right?" He uttered this last word in a confident tone, as if he were suggesting that he could not be wrong on this point, but on the inside his tone was much different. On the inside he was saying, *Help me. Help me, anyone. Please, someone help me.* And for some reason he made eye contact with Eileen O'Neill.

"I think I understand what you're getting at," she said.

*Of course you do,* Watkins thought.

"You were trying to make us feel what Jim Washington might have felt when Tony called him a gorilla."

"Yes! Thank you," Watkins exclaimed. "You see, everyone, that's all I was trying to do. As your parents might have said, 'I did it for your own good.'"

"I can see that, too. But I have a question." It was Jessica. The brief respite provided by Eileen O'Neill quickly evaporated. Up to this point Watkins might have allowed himself to suspect that the class, especially Theodore, had simply been tormenting him. But with Jessica now involved, Watkins braced for a killer question.

"What if Tony Falcone said 'I really didn't mean anything by my comment. I wasn't attacking anyone. I was only trying to make a point'?"

"But this is a very different situation," Watkins retorted immediately and then realized that his defense rested on a contradiction. "I mean it's similar in that you probably had the same feelings that Washington had. But it's different in that I don't really think you're stupid and lazy." His voice trailed off at the end.

"So," Jessica asked, "should we judge your comments on what you meant or how we felt?"

For the past several minutes Watkins had been moving around the front of the room and at this point found himself standing behind the teacher's desk. At Jessica's question, he pulled the desk chair out and sat down. After looking blankly at the class for a few silent moments, he finally said, "Wow, you guys are good. You're very good." A few of the students smiled.

"You don't really mean that, do you?" Pete Churnip asked.

Watkins let his shoulders fall forward until his forehead rested on the desk. The class laughed. He sat up. "Okay, okay." He stood and drew a line down the center of the chalkboard. On one side he scribbled "harassment" and on the other "my methods."

"What does that say?" someone asked. "My mother?"

"My methods. My methods," Watkins answered, repairing the "e." "Can I get a break in here today, or what?" he said smiling. "Let me start by saying that I'm sorry if I upset anyone. I certainly didn't mean to. Perhaps you think I went too far."

"Well, I think some teachers do go too far in trying to prove a point," Belinda volunteered. "I saw on one of those news shows that a teacher somewhere had, like, a guy with a gun come into his class and, you know, pretend to rob the teacher. I would have been so angry if that happened in a class I was in."

"Why?" Watkins asked, grateful that the focus was now off him and onto other teachers. The conversation should flow more smoothly, he reasoned.

"Because I would have been scared!" she replied as if the question were stupid. "No one in the class knew it was, you know, set up by the teacher. I'll bet some students were very afraid."

"I've heard about similar incidents," Watkins said. "I think in that case the professor was trying to show that eyewitnesses to a crime don't always tell the same story. They don't always give the same description to police. Some of the students saw a tall man, some saw a short one, some saw blonde hair, some saw brown. Their fear and shock interfered with their ability to see things clearly. That sounds like a good lesson."

"You can learn it other ways, doncha think?" Belinda responded.

"I suppose you can," Watkins responded. "But why wouldn't you say that although you were upset as part of the experiment, it was, objectively speaking, an effective way to make a point that perhaps couldn't be made simply by expressing it. Now you know what it feels like to be called names. Could you have gotten that feeling if I'd come in and said, 'It doesn't feel good to be harassed verbally'?"

"That reminds me of something we read about in my Sociology class," Meagan Hjelm said. This guy was trying to see how much people would listen to authorities. So he kept telling them to give electric shocks to people."

"Milgram," Watkins said.

"Yeah that was him. I'd have zapped *him* if he did that to me. That was mean to do that to people."

Watkins at first couldn't see the connection, but after some thought he said, "You think he went too far in trying to prove a point?"

"Yes, I do," Meagan replied. I felt very sorry for the people in that experiment."

"You know, Professor Watkins, you said, 'objectively speaking' just a minute ago. I forget what it was about." The comment came from Jen Wiener.

"Yes, about judging if the experiment was effective or not. I said that you might be able to say objectively that something was good, effective—like an experiment—even though personally it bothered or even upset you."

"Yeah, that was it. But I think it's impossible to judge unless you *have* been involved. If I know what it's like to be abused, then I can say no one should be abused. I can be more objective, if that makes any sense. Do you know what I'm trying to say?"

He slumped back until he was half sitting on the desk. Not only did he know, he started to feel that same sick feeling come over him that he'd felt at Jessica's question. He had begun the class attempting to get them to feel the pain of others, specifically the pain Jim Washington may experienced hearing Tony's words, even though Tony's intentions were good. Now he seemed to be arguing that people could be detached and mathematical, seeing the value in experiments despite how painful they might be for the subjects. *What exactly are you doing?* he wondered. *How did you get here? What* do *you believe?* He started to feel as if he'd separated into two entities, one sitting like a ventriloquist's dummy in front of nineteen students waiting for him to come alive, the other floating somewhere near the ceiling, looking at the dummy and asking, "What are you doing down there? You're making no sense. You're babbling. Go home. Run." *No wonder these kids get confused sometimes,* he thought. He blew out his cheeks and sighed long and loudly, a sight at which several students giggled. He stood, looked at his scheme on the board, then at the class, at the board, at the class.

"Yes, I do, Jen," he finally replied. "I know what you mean, and you've said it quiet well. In fact, that's what I was trying to show at the start of class—that unless you've been there, you might not know what it's like. I think that sometimes true objectivity depends on our having lived through the same experiences, pains, joys, sorrows, triumphs of the people we are judging. You're right. Of course, that's not always the case, wouldn't you say? We can evaluate a movie without ever having made one. But sometimes in judging the behaviors or the reactions of others, it helps to have walked in their shoes, or at least imagine what it must be like to be that person." Watkins looked at John, but John appeared not to be listening.

"What about murder?" Ann Marie asked. "Isn't that always wrong?"

"Well, no," Watkins responded, 'I'd say that in some cases, there are moral absolutes. I can't think of a situation when certain behaviors—abusing a child, for example—are warranted. But even in judging a murder, we'd probably want to know the circumstances. Perhaps if an abused woman kills her husband, another woman who has suffered abuse may be more likely to understand the motivation behind the killing. Or how about in judging the actions of a man who had, say, premeditatedly walked up behind Hitler and shot him in the head. Would the world have judged him as a criminal or savior? How would a Jew have judged him?"

"Good question," Pete Churnip said.

"Thank you," Watkins responded, grinning. "Here's the point, I think." He rolled his eyes. "I think that when judging a situation or event or person, you must consider so many particulars, such as the time, place, people involved, history, intention, effect, and so on. And you can still say, after considering all those circumstances, that an event or situation should never have occurred or that a person was wrong in committing a certain act. Considering all the factors involved doesn't mean that I can never pass judgment. If I set down the criteria and consider the context, I can make an evaluation. I think the ability to establish guidelines and criteria comes from having a good head on your shoulders, but I think the ability to consider the context comes from having a good and sensitive heart. In other words, you have to have a good heart—in this case a capacity for empathy—to know that saying "gorilla" to an African-American man might be insulting. You have to be willing to look at the big picture, step out of yourself, take everything into focus, consider every angle, avoid quick conclusions. Is this making any sense?"

"Is this going to be on the test?" Gary Kardell asked, rubbing his forehead. "I'm starting to get a headache."

Some students laughed, but a scattering of nods encouraged Watkins to continue. "I should tell you at this point that Tony called me, and I asked him what happened. He told me that members of the team often call each other animal names."

"I've heard that's true," Matthew said.

"So," Watkins continued, "in judging this event, we would need to know Tony's reasons and Jim's reaction. It's possible that despite what Tony may have intended, his comments could have been insensitive and may have offended Jim Perhaps Tony should apologize to Jim, if Jim wants an apology. Fair enough?"

"I think so," Jessica said.

"I do, too," several others responded. And several students nodded their agreement.

"Okay, then," Watkins continued. "Here's where I think we are. In judging any situation, we need to consider everything and everyone involved. Evaluating something means looking at the entire context, including intentions, motives, reactions, consequences"—he was writing all this on the board—"history, experience, and so forth. And we'd need to gather as much information about an event or situation as we possibly could. You couldn't just take one person's word."

"I was going to say that," Ann Marie exclaimed. "People lie. You can't really know their intentions."

"Or their reactions," Pete Churnip added. "Someone could say, 'Oh, I was terribly hurt by what was said,' but maybe they're really not."

"Which is why it would be important to gather as much evidence as possible. We are more likely to believe a person if their history bears them out—character witnesses, you might say."

"Okay," Pete returned, "say someone is really sensitive and they're at a party and they spill something. Say this person is large. Okay, they spill something on someone else and that other person says, "You cow."

"Staying with the animal theme," Watkins said.

Pete laughed. "Yeah, poor animals; they probably hate being dragged down like this. Okay, you're standing there and you overhear it. What would you say about this?"

"To the people involved?!" Watkins knew himself well enough to know that he would say nothing at all, that he'd pretend not to have noticed.

"No, just what would you say about this situation?"

"Well," Watkins said, pausing to think, "I'd say that the comment was probably just an immediate reaction, but that it was insensitive whether the, uh, spiller was large or small and that the spillee owes the spiller an apology. But it's possible that the 'the cow' is not at all offended and might say, 'Yeah, I'm a cow, clumsy me, sorry. Where's the club soda?' In that case, no harm done."

"But don't call people cows," Eileen reminded the class.

"Okay, what if they both left immediately?" Pete asked. "What if you couldn't tell how either felt. Couldn't you judge the situation just on what you saw?"

"Am I alone on this one?" Watkins asked the class. "Doesn't anyone want to help me here?"

"You're on your own, Professor," Theodore said in a friendly tone. "You started it."

"Thanks," Watkins returned. "All right, going with what we've said this morning, I would try to imagine what both parties were thinking and how they felt. It's not pleasant to have something spilled on you, and so I could see why that person blurted out "you cow." But that's not a nice thing to hear, so I would assume the person called that would be hurt. I'd say they owe each other an apology. But my sympathies would lie more with the person called a cow—not so much because of his size, but because it was probably an accident—so I'd say that person gets a hardier apology. Case closed? I can tell by your look that you don't agree, Theodore."

"You're being too nice."

"Too nice?! How would you handle it?" Watkins asked.

"The way I always do in those situations." He paused and then yelled out, "Food fight!" Several students laughed.

"How do you know it was an accident?" Jessica asked.

"Pardon me," Watkins said.

"How do you know that the spiller didn't deliberately try to ruin the other person's clothes? Maybe he's been plotting this apparently accidental spilling for months." She said this in the manner of a sitcom detective, slowly enunciating every syllable of "apparently accidental."

Gary Kardell groaned loudly from the back of the room. "Oh, my head. Please stop. It's going to explode."

"*I'm* starting to get a headache," Watkins replied, laughing and rubbing his eyebrows with the pads of his fingers. "Look, Jessica. Stop making trouble. It was an accident. Period."

Watkins knew that this would be a good time to end the period and start the weekend, but he'd brought something to share with them, and he was determined to fulfill that mission. "It occurs to me," he said, "that Pete's question is pretty good. How would you judge a case if you knew nothing about the parties involved, if you didn't know their intentions or feelings? Say that all you had to go on was that Person A, who is white, called Person B, who is black, a "gorilla." And say that incident occurred on campus. Is Person A guilty of committing an act of hate speech? Has he violated the college code?"

"What is the college code?" Pete asked.

"I'm glad you asked," Watkins responded, picking up the manila folder he had tossed on the desk forty minutes earlier. After distributing the handout, he read:

Wexford College Student Handbook
Part 3: Student Behavior
Section V: Hate Speech

In order to ensure that all students, staff, faculty, administrators and guests of Wexford College may work and study in an environment free of humiliation, indignity, discomfort and fear, the College will not tolerate actions or language that a reasonable person would conclude victimizes an individual or group on the basis of gender, race, ethnicity or national origin, religion or creed, sexual orientation, age, or handicap. Specifically, the College will take disciplinary action against anyone exhibiting the following behaviors on College-owned property: participating in events deemed offensive to individuals and groups (for example, "slave auctions" or "wet T-shirt contests"); creating a hostile educational environment or threatening a student's academic efforts; taunting; threatening violence against a person or group; using "fighting words" (words intended to provoke violent confrontation); publishing or distributing obscenity; defaming or libeling; advocating discrimination or hatred (for example, distributing leaflets for a supremacy group); or creating mental duress.

"Whew," one student whistled.
"Wow!" another said.
Several of the students fidgeted and looked at one another as if they'd just discovered that all privileges had been revoked.
"I had no idea this even existed," Jen said.
"Publishing or distributing obscenity," Chris read, perhaps unwittingly, out loud in a flat tone.
"Don't worry, Chris, you can still use the Internet. Just don't scan any pictures of yourself," Pete said.
Chris looked up. "Professor Watkins, Pete is taunting me. I'd like him thrown out of school."

Amid the laughing, one student who hadn't said anything to this point, spoke up. "Hey, what ever happened to free speech?"

"I think that's a good question," Watkins returned; "but it may be beyond our abilities right now to determine whether the school's code violates the first amendment, and besides, as a private college, we have a little more leeway."

"You know," Belinda said, "I like these rules. I'd like to see the school, you know, *really* enforce them."

Hoping secretly that she could do so briefly and with fluid sentences, Watkins asked her to elaborate.

"Well, like, for one thing, you know these shirts the guys wear?"

She asked the question as if Watkins would immediately recognize the reference, but he didn't. "What shirts?"

"You knowww," Belinda replied, trying to communicate her thoughts telepathically. "You know, the ones with the, you know."

"Big Dick's Bar and Grill," Theodore volunteered without hesitation or stammer.

"Thank you, Theodore," Watkins said. "What would I do without you?"

"No problem."

Watkins invited Belinda to continue.

"Okay, well, those shirts, I think they should be against the rules."

"You find them offensive?" Watkins asked.

"Very," she replied.

Ann Marie concurred. And so did Meagan.

"What's the problem?" Theodore insisted on knowing.

"False advertising," came Meagan's immediate response.

As the class roared, Watkins felt the blood rush up his neck, over his cheeks and into his forehead. But the joke was a good one, and he laughed.

"Hey, Teddy," Chris said, "she's heard about you."

"What's everyone looking at me for," Theodore responded. "I don't have one." He quickly added "a T-shirt like that, I mean," but it was far too late, the eruption of laughter blurring that phrase and for the next several moments obscuring whatever else it was he was trying to say.

As the class caught its breath, Watkins stifled his own amusement and looked at Theodore to make sure he was surviving the embarrassment. "Okay, okay," was all he could think of to say, and when the class finally quieted, he looked at Theodore. "We know what you were trying to say. Words are tricky things, aren't they." Maybe because he agreed, Theodore just looked silently at Watkins and nodded.

Knowing that returning to a serious conversation would be difficult, Watkins tried anyway: "Okay, everyone, let's get back to this question. Did Tony violate this code?" No one seemed particularly eager to volunteer. In fact, the silence was broken only by a few students closing their notebooks and reaching for their bags, reminding him of his promise.

"All right," he said. "I did say you could go early." He asked that they answer the question for homework by examining Tony's actions as reported in the newspaper and wished them a good weekend with their parents. "Remember to hide your T-shirts, and whatever you do, don't spill anything." Some students laughed politely, but most raced for the door. As he erased the board he heard at his back a student say his name.


### *Eileen*


"Professor Watkins?"

"Yes, Eileen. Oh, yeah, your paper." Watkins told her that he'd left it in his office and invited her to walk there with him to get it. As they walked the few flights of stairs, Watkins asked how things were going.

"Oh, fine," she responded quietly.

"I remember at the beginning you didn't think you'd stick with it. I'm glad you changed your mind."

"I've enjoyed it," Eileen replied. "I like the class discussions."

"Oh, by the way," Watkins said, "thanks for coming to my defense this morning. It was getting lonely up there."

*Lonely?* Eileen thought. She didn't expect such a personal revelation from Watkins. This was a word she understood, but she'd always assumed that teachers were—and believed themselves to be—in complete control of the classroom. To her, teachers were never apprehensive or nervous, never shy, never distressed, never lonely. Sure, they made mistakes, cracked bad jokes, lost their place sometimes, were distracted by thoughts of their families or other responsibilities, looked foolish or out-of-touch, but that they *felt* lonely or needed defending in a room full of youngsters with high school diplomas—that she never expected. She was genuinely surprised.

"I don't remember saying anything."

"When I was trying to explain why I'd been calling everyone names, you said you understood what I was trying to do."

"Huh, compared to all the really smart things people said today, my comments weren't much."

"Sometimes it's not what you say; it's that you say anything. It's great just to get a little help when you're up there."

*"Up there? That's the second time he said that,* Eileen thought, fascinated that Watkins apparently saw himself as being on display or maybe on stage. "Oh, I should have said more. I think it was a good point you were making. At first I didn't know why you called us lazy and stupid. But you did make me realize how Jim might have felt. I think some of those kids were just giving you a hard time. I saw the point, though."

"You're probably one student who doesn't need the lesson," Watkins said.

"Not true," Eileen replied. "I have a lot to learn about how other people feel."

They had reached the office door. "Well, your paper really showed a wonderful sensitivity. I enjoyed reading it," Watkins said. When he opened the door, Watkins was clearly surprised to see a box sitting on his desk. "Yea," he said; "they finally found my stuff. I set this box outside my office door when I first got here in September," Watkins explained, "and went to get my office key. While I was gone, Maintenance picked it up thinking it was trash." He opened the box and took out an official looking document in a black frame. A thick crack ran diagonally across the glass.

"My degree," said Watkins.

"They broke it," Eileen said sympathetically.

"It was like that," Watkins replied. He unpacked a few other items from the box—a coffee-stained mug with a Baltimore Orioles logo; a Styrofoam cup with about twenty pencils, most of which were the length of Eileen's little finger and had no eraser left on them; a half dozen postcards with so many thumbtack holes they looked as if Watkins had used them as dart boards, a stapler, a tangle of rubber bands and paper clips, a small terra cotta pot with hardened soil and the withered remains of a spider plant, a half roll of scotch tape, and a desk lamp with no bulb. Watkins stood looking at the collection on his desk, which reminded Eileen of a table at a flea market. Finally he looked at Eileen. "How could Maintenance be so dumb?" he wondered out loud.

Eileen laughed.

"Well, here's your paper. I read it as a draft and made some comments for improving it. If you need me to explain anything further, let me know."

Eileen thanked him and left the office. Walking down the stairs, she read Watkins's comment.

> Eileen,
> Once again, your writing has left me speechless. The love and compassion you show toward your sister here, the under-standing, the sense of humor, the depth of emotion—all make this draft one of the most impressive I've seen all semester. Your writing is so candid and genuine that you give your reader a wonderful sense of who you are and what you believe and feel. I've made some suggestions in the margins for im-proving your essay. When you have made those changes, please submit your essay for a grade. (By the way, the Writing Lab may be able to offer you some help in improving your work.)

Deciding to take Watkins's advice, Eileen immediately headed for the Writing Lab, where she spent half an hour with a tutor before leaving campus for the day. She drove for about five minutes thinking about Watkins standing over his belongings and turned on the radio. She had started finding the shock jock doc amusing, and as usual, Dr. Sally was solving the most profound and complicated problems with slogans and thirty seconds of analysis: To a caller contemplating marriage but wondering if she should demand that her boyfriend pay more attention to her before agreeing to wed: "Deciding to marry a man is like buying a car; you have to push them to the limit during the test drive. You wouldn't want to buy a car that couldn't handle faster speeds on the highway, would you?"

To a caller who wanted to know whether she should trust her father as a babysitter, when her father had failed at the job once in the past: "Why would you throw a child into an alligator pit when you know that alligators eat children?"

To a caller whose parents had died and whose girlfriend was pregnant: "And now you want to become a baby-killer? Hasn't there been enough death in your family? What kind of man are you?"

To a mother who said she must work to supplement her husband's meager income: "Your child isn't going to be better off because you're driving a Lexus and eating caviar in a few years."

The callers, of course, were no better at reasoning. One claimed that she saw nothing wrong with single women having children. "Many very intelligent women—professors, Broadway actresses, scientists—have done it," she claimed in defense of her decision. Another revealed that she insisted that her boyfriend buy her a diamond. "I told myself, 'If he doesn't buy me one, I'll know he doesn't love me,'" she said. "But he bought me one, so I know he loves me very much."

After a few minutes more, Eileen decided she'd had enough and was about to change the station, when the sheer coincidence of one of Sally's comments stopped her: "People must exhibit total control of their feelings," she said spitting out the word "feelings" as if it were kerosene. "They must learn to be free of their emotions and feelings and to fight any urge that would cause them to abandon the right course of action. Our understanding of the difference between right and wrong must inform our decisions. Our emotions can lead us to make fatally wrong decisions." To illustrate the point, Sally claimed that parents who had grown apart and who claimed to no longer love one another must remain together for the sake of the children. "Their feelings for one another are secondary; they'll learn to love again if they stay together."

In class Eileen had listened to Watkins discuss—and maybe discover for himself—the connection between feeling and thought and the place of emotions in making decisions and forming judgments. And yet here was someone who seemed to be arguing the very opposite of what her professor believed. Eileen concentrated hard on remembering the doctor's words. She thought she might tell Watkins what he was missing.

### John

Though he never participated in class discussions, John usually listened intently to the opinions of his classmates, often recording their ideas in his notebook and sometimes even responding to them in short, written comments. "That's dumb," he'd write next to something he disagreed with or "Yes" near an opinion that reflected his own. Today, however he had listened very little and written nothing. Distracted by two competing thoughts—his mother's visit for Parents' Weekend and his conversation with Nick—he spent most of the class time doodling in his notebook and wondering why he had come to college in the first place. John played the dialogue over and over in his mind.

*    *    *

"Jen says you just sat there like you were deaf and blind. Left her hanging. She says she was trying to get you to help, but you just ignored her. How could you do that? How could you not say something when you knew she wanted you to help her out?"

John could think of no defense but ignorance. "I wasn't really listening, Nick. I didn't know what was going on."

"Bullshit!" Nick nearly screamed. "Don't lie, John. You were listening. You always listen. You just never speak. I thought we were friends. This was your chance to stand up for something. I know how you *feel* about things, I've been your roommate for almost two months. But it's not enough. What's wrong? Why don't you speak up?"

John's first impulse was to leave the room. He felt the desire to cry rolling up from his chest, but he controlled himself. After a few moments, he finally said, "I'm afraid."

"Afraid of what? What's there to be afraid of?" Nick might have been solicitous, but John heard only condemnation and ridicule in Nick's tone. He stood up and made a motion toward the door. Nick grabbed his arm. "Where you going, John?"

"Anywhere."

"What's going on? What's wrong?" Nick's tone was now inarguably soft, parental. John could feel Nick's muscular fingers around his skinny forearm.

"I'm, uh, I'm, I don't know, I'm . . ." John knew what he wanted to say, but he couldn't find the words.

"You're not afraid of me, are you, John?"

John looked at Nick's hand. "Well, not usually."

Nick laughed and loosened his grip. "I'm sorry. Now tell me, please, what's going on."

The dam burst. "I don't know what I'm afraid of. I'm afraid of everything. I'm afraid I'll be wrong or sound stupid or that everyone will start laughing at me or hate me or think I'm a jerk or that I won't be able to think of the words and I'll start stammering or that people will look at me or . . ."

"Whoa, John, I have class this afternoon," Nick said laughing. "I thought you told me at the beginning of the semester—you remember, that time I used you for target practice in tennis—you told me you wouldn't worry so much about what people thought about you."

"I stopped worrying so much of what *you* thought about me, but I guess I should have thought more about what you think, as it turns out. Now I've pissed you off."

"It's not about me, John. Listen, it's a delicate balance. You have to consider other people's impressions of you. You don't want to pull out a sandwich during a job interview. You don't want to insult people because you don't care about their feelings. You don't want to be a jerk who thinks the universe revolves around him. But, John, you're not a jerk. You're a great guy with a terrific brain and a good heart. Who wouldn't like you, except for me right now? But don't worry about that. I'll get over it."

Nick was grinning. John couldn't fight it any longer. The tears ran down his checks. "You're a great friend, Nick. I'm sorry. I'm sorry I didn't support Jen in class. I'll be a better friend next time."

John could see that Nick wasn't exactly sure what to do with a blubbery male friend. Nick reached over and gave John two quick and somewhat forceful slaps on the upper arm. "Don't worry about it," he said. "We just need to get you more involved. You don't want to watch your life pass you by, do you? You can't always be just a spectator. Sometimes you gotta swing."

"You're not going to make me play sports, are you?" John asked half joking.

"Nah," Nick responded; "I wouldn't do that to myself."

The conversation continued for another two hours, John revealing for the first time the story of his childhood, his debilitating shyness in high school, his lack of any experience with women. He talked and Nick listened like no counselor, RA, therapist, psychologist, parent or teacher ever had or could. Nick's life of affluence and participation had been entirely different, but the sympathy and understanding he demonstrated made John feel that they'd grown up in the same household. At the end of the afternoon, John felt that he'd discovered a long-lost brother, and he vowed to Nick to speak up for what he believed in and to support Jen as if she were one of the family.

*   *   *

So here he sat on Thursday quietly doodling in his notebook and missing every chance to say something, even a chance to comment on his own notion that you didn't have to experience everything if you had an imagination. Watkins had tossed him the ball, underhand and slow, and he'd stood there with the bat on his shoulder.

At the end of class, John hurried from the room to catch up with Jen. "Jen, I'm sorry I was so quiet today. I've got a lot on my mind."

Jen seemed confused. "Huh," she said. "Oh, don't worry about it. I've got a lot on my mind, too. My parents are coming for the week-end, and I never told them about Nick."

# CHAPTER IV

# Saturday, October 25
## Parents' Weekend

### John

As it turned out, Jen needn't have worried. On Friday, Nick's brother-in-law was taken to the hospital for an emergency appendectomy, and Nick went home to help his sister for the few days her husband needed to recuperate. On Saturday morning he called John to say that the surgery went well and that he'd be back Monday morning, which left John to enjoy Parents' Weekend without his new best friend. About ten minutes after Nick's call, John heard a knock at the door. When he opened it his old best friend fell upon him as if a gale wind had blown up behind her.

John's mother held his face in both hands and kissed his cheeks and forehead as she had since he was five years old. "Johnny, Oh, I miss you. I miss my baby."

"Mom," John pleaded, "come into the room. Please." She stepped inside still holding on to his face. "Besides, Mom, I saw you a few weeks ago and talk to you almost every day."

"That doesn't matter to a mother," she countered. "I miss you the minute I hang up the phone."

They sat in John's room catching up. Mom talked about work and her friends. John talked about school and Nick. Out of paranoia, Jen had hidden even the picture of her and Nick that sat on the desk, so John's mother hadn't a clue what he looked like, but after half an hour she knew that he was bright, athletic, handsome, fun-loving, talkative, compassionate, sensitive, nurturing, honest, moral, and even neat. John saw her looking around the room in disbelieve. "Not that kind of neat. I mean he dresses nicely, smells good."

John's mother looked worried. "Have you met any nice girls, John?"

John laughed. "Mom! Don't be ridiculous!" he said and went on to assure her that his relationship with Nick was purely platonic, "though he does have a nice butt."

"Oh, John!" his mother said, blushing and laughing. Then after a few moments, "So have you met any nice girls?"

"Well, I've met one, but she hasn't met me."

For the rest of the day, John showed his mother the campus, his classrooms, the library, the cafeteria. At the football game they watched the Cardinals lose by 21 points, even though Jim Washington caught six passes for 130 yards. When the defense took the field, John watched Tony Falcone and Jim stand together on the sidelines. With their helmets and face masks, he couldn't see their expressions, but their body language suggested to John that these two men bore no animosity between them. At 6:00 John stood outside his dorm room while his mother freshened up and changed into a simple black dress for the evening's dinner dance. "I'm sorry to put you out like this. I should have gotten a hotel room," she said to John when she stepped out of the room, as if paying for one would have been no problem for her. "How do I look?"

Since childhood, John had complimented his mother on her appearance, sometimes out of habit and sometimes because, like tonight, she was truly beautiful. It occurred to him that though she was almost forty, she could easily pass as his slightly older sister or even as his date. He bristled slightly at the thought, but then realized that he wouldn't mind too much if anyone assumed that this shapely, dark, beautiful woman was his girlfriend. "Incredible," he said. "Just incredible."

At dinner they sat with Jen and her parents and with one of Jen's friends and her parents. The friend was in John's history class, but she acted as if they'd never met, upsetting him until he realized that without his cap he may look different to her and that since he never said a word in class except on the first day, no one had ever looked in his direction. He ate most of the meal looking at his plate, but his mother participated excitedly in the conversation at the table.

When dinner ended, the DJ started the evening's music with, predictably, "Sunrise, Sunset," and his mother insisted that he dance with her. He hated dancing because of the way everyone in the room stopped what they were doing to watch and ridicule his clumsy attempt at rhythmic movement. "You know, you dance very well," his mother assured him. But when the slow song ended and "Twist and Shout" started, John didn't care how flattering his mother was, he wanted off the floor—now. He couldn't, however, disappoint his mother, who danced gracefully to any music and seemed happier now than John could remember. So twisting through an arc of about ten degrees, his fists clenched, his arms bent at forty-five degrees and rigid, he scanned the room for spectators. With everyone else safely involved in their own geometries, John relaxed and allowed himself to twist a few degrees more in each direction. In his mind he was working out a deal with his mother: if he got through this, he would use it to bargain his way out of dancing to "YMCA," "The Chicken Dance," or "The Macarena," or any of the other embarrassing romps his mother participated in at weddings and graduation parties.

He was twisting to the second verse and adding "Hot Hot Hot" to his list when the worst possible thing happened. John spotted Eileen O'Neill standing at the periphery of all these foolish dancers, talking to someone whom John prayed was her father. They were talking, he was certain, about the ridiculous looking couple in the center of the room still dancing even though the music had stopped and everyone else had left the floor. He twisted quickly to his left and froze. When the haze lifted, he realized he was still surrounded by gyrating parents and their offspring. He moved to position his back to Eileen and kept dancing, praying for a power outage or a cracked CD. When the song ended he briskly walked ahead of his mother back to the table.

"What's wrong?" she asked, apparently having noticed how profusely he sweated for not having danced very enthusiastically. "Are you getting sick?"

*What a brilliant idea, Mom*, he thought and asked for a glass of soda. Promising to return immediately, she left the table, returning about ten minutes later.

"I'm so sorry, honey, " she said. "I got talking to a very charming, handsome man near the bar." She handed John the glass. "He asked me to dance. I'll just dance one with him, sweetheart. Are you feeling any better?"

"Yes, you have a good time," John said showing some agony but secretly delighted that his mother had found someone else to torture. She skipped away from the table, but John didn't watch her. He couldn't bear to watch his mother and some old guy dancing to "Old Time Rock and Roll," so he just sat hunched over, holding his glass a few inches off the table and focusing on the ginger ale he was sucking though a straw, a distraction that provided very little entertainment until he started blowing bubbles into the drink.

"John, isn't it? I think you're in my writing class."

John looked up, his glass in hand, the straw still clenched between his lips, and Eileen O'Neill looking directly into his eyes.

He said "Hi," but because he gasped at the same time, the word seemed to be going backward and at a much higher pitch than it would have normally sounded had it been going forward. The straw fell from his lips and he let the glass slip from his hand to the table, where the force of the impact propelled several droplets of soda onto his face. He wiped them away with his hand and said "Hi" again in a voice somewhat closer to the one he usually used.

"Mind if I sit down?" Eileen asked.

"No, no," John said. Immediately worried she might think he meant "no, please don't," he got emphatic about what he did mean: "I mean 'no' I don't mind, I mean not at all, yes, yes, I mean yes, please, please sit down, sit down."

"Well, if you insist," she responded in what John prayed to God was not meant to be a mocking tone.

"Your mother is a gorgeous woman," Eileen said.

"How do you know my mother?" John asked.

"She's dancing with my father."

John couldn't tell if he was truly about to throw up or if the feeling that swept over him was simply the result of failing to breathe. He began to stammer partly because of nerves and partly because he could think of absolutely nothing to say. "I, uh, uh, I, uh, you, uh, you, my mother, she, uh, she."

"She what?"

"She likes to dance."

Eileen said nothing for a moment as she watched her father and John's mother. "Oh, you can see that. She's so energetic. And very sexy."

"Well, I wouldn't know anything about that," John said as if he'd been accused of the unspeakable.

"Oh, c'mon. You can't say whether your mother is sexy? I think my father is."

"Well, women can say those things and get away with it," John replied.

"Don't generalize and stereotype, John. What would Watkins think? Hey, did you know he was here?"

"Who?"

"Watkins."

"NO!" John insisted.

"Wow, John, you look downright scared."

"I mean, no, you're kidding, get out of here." John thought it was a smooth recovery.

"Yes, he's right over there, near the bar." She pointed him out. John could feel his chest tighten.

"Are you okay, John?" Eileen asked.

"Yeah, I just need a drink."

"Well, let's get one at the bar. We'll say hello to Watkins."

### Watkins

On Saturday afternoon, Watkins sat watching a football game on television and reading over and over a postcard he'd received in the mail from Diane:

> Pete—
> Got your letter. You're right—been in the library every day with RIDGE. I was glad to hear from you. Thanks for the warnings, though I still think I'll tell people I have a degree—if I ever get it. My advisor likes the chapters on S.T.C. Keep your fingers crossed. Talk to you soon. D.

*Ridge?! Ridge?! Not Ridge Rowlands! How could she? A guy like that! Soap opera name and a personality to match. Ridge? A few more of those soap opera names and they could start their own National Park. Stone, Thorn, Brooke, Ridge. How could she? RIDGE? He couldn't read a piece of literature to save his life. And an Americanist! They'll never make it! And she capitalizes his name! What's with that?!*

Watkins tossed the postcard on the floor and tried to nap on the futon. When the phone rang, he let the machine record the call, which he could tell came from his mother since there was silence for about ten seconds after the beep, followed by the phone disconnecting. *Did she think that if she actually spoke to the machine, her son would somehow use the tape against her, like playing it on the six o'clock news?* he wondered. Unable to sleep comfortably because of Ridge, Watkins went for a drive and returned around 5:30 to dress for dinner. Like several other untenured faculty, he had volunteered to advise a few student clubs, and in gratitude they had ruined his Saturday evening by inviting him to meet their parents.

He could not have been more wrong about the ruining part. The evening turned out to be enormously satisfying as several parents told him how their son or daughter had mentioned him as a "great" or "interesting" teacher. "My daughter speaks rather highly of you," one parent said, using language and a tone that seemed alien to her but which she probably thought appropriate for the occasion and Watkins's stature. Watkins returned the gesture: "Your daughter is quite a fine young woman. I positively enjoy her presence in my classroom." With his luck he knew that this same woman, seeing him at some future school function, would forget herself and exclaim loudly in the presence of the Dean and the department Chair, "Do you remember me, Professor? You had my daughter!"

During the few moments when he wasn't entertaining parents, Watkins spoke to one of his colleagues, Mike Butler, an assistant math professor who had already built a reputation as one of the better teachers and an exceptional athlete. They talked for a few moments about baseball and the recent series, when the conversation turned to golf. Somehow Watkins, a good listener with a rudimentary knowledge of golf, managed to give the impression that he played the game.

"Hey," Mike said enthusiastically; "tomorrow is supposed to be a beautiful day. Want to get out early and drive a few golf balls?"

"Sounds great," Watkins returned. They set up a time and place.

Watkins had just finished speaking to an especially gracious and captivating set of parents when he was approached by Eileen O'Neill and John Zajaczkiewicz. "Hello, Professor," Eileen said in a cheery voice.

Watkins greeted them both and began talking, mostly to Eileen, about how their evening was going. He was just shouting the words "Did your parents come with you" when Bob Seger stopped singing, leaving the last few words loud enough to be heard by pretty much everyone within twenty yards of their little triangle. It may have been what attracted two more people to the group.

"Here he is! Dad, this is Professor Watkins, my writing teacher."

They exchanged greetings, and Watkins looked at John's mother. John stood like a statue.

"I'm Joyce Zajaczkiewicz," John's mother said. "My friends call me Joy."

*I can see why,* Watkins thought. "How do you do?" he said, gently shaking her hand. He started to feel a bit conspicuous in this circle of attractive people, so he tried to shift the focus from himself.

"What do you do, Mr. O'Neill?" he asked.

"I'm sorry. Please, call me Jack. I'm a carpenter."

Watkins thought immediately of Jack O'Neill bringing a hammer down onto a piece of rolled up newspaper with a mouse wrapped in it. "Oh, yes, that's a great profession. Me, I can't hammer a nail straight or crooked. I'd be lucky to make contact with it." He paused for a moment, but no else spoke. "How about you, Joy?"

"I can swing a hammer if I have to."

Watkins felt his face redden, but he laughed with the others. "I meant besides that, what do you do?"

"I work at our local library."

"Oh, a librarian, that's wonderful," Watkins said.

"Well, not exactly a librarian," she corrected him. "The *real* librarians," she said raising her eyebrows, a gesture that made her even more beautiful and caused Watkins to miss the rest of her sentence, "something, something, something."

The others had been listening and laughed. "I only help out with the children's books mostly."

Eileen's father offered to get drinks for everyone and after taking orders, he invited John to give him a hand. Together they walked toward the bar.

"Was your husband able to make it tonight, Joy?" Watkins asked in his friendliest voice.

"My husband?" Joy returned, clearly astonished.

"Yes, John wrote in his first essay that your husband is a decorated state trooper."

"A state trooper!" Joy seemed shocked and even a little embarrassed. "Oh, that's a good one!" She looked at the floor and then directly at Watkins, who assumed from her drawing a deep breath that she was summoning her strength. In hindsight, he realized she may have been stifling her laughter.

"Professor, my husband was anything but a state trooper. He may be *running* from them, but he's not one. He walked out of our lives over ten years ago, and we haven't seen or heard from him since. I'd like to *see* him so that I could have him arrested for not paying a dime of child support."

Watkins was stunned. "I, um, I'm sorry" was all he could think of to say, though he had plenty more on his mind. John had lied to him. And Joy was single.

"Don't be," Joy said. "My life's been a lot better in the past ten years. John's had the harder time. It always embarrassed him that he didn't have a father, no one to teach him to play ball or fix the car. Over the years John's fictional father has been"—she counted the professions on her fingers—"a novelist living in Paris, an engineer building dams in Uganda, a professional hockey player in Manitoba, a CIA agent in New Mexico, a jazz musician on tour, and a Navy sailor stationed at various times in Guam or Hawaii or Xanadu."

"Xanadu?"

"He was reading some poem for English class at the time. His father sometimes became a character in whatever he was reading."

"I take it he was never in Australia or Iceland."

"Only in books. Did he tell you he was running for city council at home?"

"No, I don't remember that one," Watkins said, looking at Eileen and shrugging.

"Maybe he lost the election," Eileen said, shrugging back.

"So you never remarried or changed your name?" Watkins asked, not sure where the question came from and immediately regretting that he'd been so rude. But Joy was as gracious as she was beautiful.

"No, I came close a few times, but a teenage boy has a way of scaring off potential fathers. I always meant to change my name, but I never got around to it."

Reminded of John, Watkins took the opportunity to change the course of the conversation. "You know, John's a very intelligent young man. And a pretty good writer."

"He's a good story-teller, as you know," Joy replied. He drove his high school teachers crazy. They could never tell what was real and what was made up. He has a great imagination."

"Who has a great imagination?" John asked, handing Eileen a club soda."

"Who do you think?" his mother responded, setting her palm lovingly on his cheek. Even in the faintly lit ballroom, Watkins could see him blushing. John turned quickly to look at Watkins.

116

"Your mother has been telling me about how creative you are, John."

"Oh, yeah, I guess," John replied stirring his soda and staring at it as if he expected to see the Titanic rise to the top.

"Well, you'll have to come to the office on Tuesday. We'll talk about how you can best use that creative mind."

John's mother agreed that the idea was excellent. "He could really use some guidance, Professor. I'm sure he'd appreciate your help, wouldn't you, John?"

"Sure. That sounds great," John replied confidently and apparently excited by the suggestion, but Watkins could see from the speed at which John had stirred his soda into flatness that he would probably spend the few days till Tuesday in a cold sweat.

"Well, I'll see you then," Watkins said looking at his watch. Eileen's father had handed John's mother a gin and tonic and was standing close by, close enough that Watkins was unable to ignore the fact that they seemed to have been designed for one another. "Oh my," Watkins said, "look at the time. I really should be going." All his life he'd been unable to extricate himself from a conversation without either making an excuse for his early departure or promising to continue the conversation at a later date. The habit normally caused trouble for him. "I'll talk to you in a few days," he'd say to his mother at the end of a phone call, which pretty much ensured that the next phone call would begin with an apology for not having called in two weeks. In the current situation, "We'll all have to talk again" would have done the trick, but Watkins had John's mendacity without his creativity. "Oh my, look at the time," he said. "I really should be going. I have a date."

"Oh," Joy sang, "a late date. Well, Professor, how nice! But, you should have brought her along."

"Uh, the invitation seemed to be for one, so I thought I'd just stay a short time. She's waiting for me."

"In the car?" Jack asked in a perfect deadpan, which started everyone laughing, including Watkins.

"Good one, Dad," Eileen said.

"She might be getting cold. I'd better go. Good night, everyone. Have fun," Watkins said and walked away smiling—on the outside, but inside he felt miserable, partly for being unable to merely leave without an excuse or apology, mostly because no one waited in his car, or in his apartment, or at a restaurant or bar or anywhere else.

"Oh, Professor Watkins," Eileen called after him. Watkins turned. "You should listen to Dr. Sally."

"The radio psychologist?" Watkins asked glumly. *Does it show that badly?* he thought.

"Yeah," Eileen replied. "Well, actually, she should listen to you."

# Sunday, October 26

Eileen poked her fork at the remnants of her scrambled eggs. *He must think I'm crazy. He probably had no idea what I meant by that. I should just keep my mouth shut.* Her mind was a collage of images from the previous evening. She cringed at the sight of Watkins staring in confusion at her last comment, but thrilled at the picture of her father dancing. In almost three years, he had enjoyed few moments of real happiness, and none of them involved a woman. She had on so many occasions told him that both she and Maury wanted him to be happy and that she was certain her grandmother felt the same way. Usually so cautious and restrained, he danced last night as if he'd finally heard the spirit of her mother say it as well.

On the drive home, she sensed his guilt. "Eileen, I have to tell you that. . . ." She stopped him.

"Dad, please don't apologize for anything. I'll support you in whatever you do."

"I know you will, and I love you for it," he said. "And what are *you* going to do?"

"About what?"

"About John Zakevik?"

"What are you suggesting?" she asked, feigning surprise.

"Well, if I'm any judge of a boy in love, he's in love."

Snapping out of her reverie, she raised the fork to her mouth but set it down before it reached her lips. She pushed the plate away and picked up her coffee cup. She remembered her first sight of John at the table. She was stunned at how handsome he was without his cap. *He looks like a younger Johnny Depp*, she remembered thinking. And he was blowing bubbles in a glass of 7-up. She didn't believe in love at first sight, but she'd never seen Johnny Depp blowing bubbles in a glass of 7-up before.

Recalling his endearing way of bumbling and stammering, she smiled and wondered what he was doing at that very moment. *Maybe he was in Tanzania or Barbados,* she thought. His storytelling didn't bother her. John may have gone too far, but she understood his desire to invent a complete family.

"Eileen! Hey, Eileen, you home? What does that taste like?"

"What does what taste like, Maury?"

"Coffee."

"Do you want to try it?"

"Can I, Dad?"

"Only if you promise you won't like it."

Maury took a mouthful of Eileen's coffee and spit it back into the cup. How you can drink that stuff?"

"It's good you don't like it," her grandmother said. "Don't ever get started on it."

Eileen's entire family seemed joyful, and she knew that their bright disposition was a reflection of her father's high spirits. He was always kind and sensitive, but this morning he seemed alive. He talked excitedly at breakfast about simple things—finding a pumpkin after breakfast, visiting his brother for Thanksgiving, fixing Eileen's car finally, and getting the house painted in the spring. "We'll let Maury pick the color," he said.

"The color of coffee," she insisted.

"With or without cream?" her father asked.

Eileen picked up her cup and drank what remained.

"Ewwwwww," Maury said.

They left the restaurant and stepped into a beautiful late October Sunday. While Eileen's father searched his pockets for quarters to buy a newspaper at a machine, Eileen read the headline through the glass. When her father opened the machine, Eileen grabbed the paper and continued reading. "Oh, poor Jim Washington," she said. "There's no way this is Tony. No way!"

"What are you talking about?" her father asked, taking the paper from her and reading.

Maury was impatient. "What's going on? What's going on, Dad?" she asked.

### Watkins

On Sunday morning, Watkins hit his snooze button a record five times, which left him ten minutes to dress and get to the driving range where Mike awaited him.

120

"Morning," Mike said, and after Watkins's profuse apology for being late, assured him that he didn't mind waiting. "No problem. I already got us each a bucket of balls. Did you bring your own club?"

"Damn!" Watkins said. "I was in such a hurry, I forgot."

"No problem. They've got plenty here." He and Watkins walked to the concession to get a club. Watkins picked up the first one he saw.

"Are you sure that one's the right size and all?" Mike asked.

"Oh, sure," Watkins replied. "I can tell by looking at it."

"For some reason, you don't see a lot of left-handed golfers," Mike said. Watkins looked at the club.

"I think I'll swing right-handed today," he said returning to the rack to get a new club. "I don't want to show anybody up," he said with a sheepish grin.

"You've driven balls before, haven't you?" Mike asked.

"Oh, sure," Watkins replied as if the question were nonsensical. He immediately remembered the one time he *had* driven a golf ball, infuriating his father: "You're going to hurt someone, Petey. Hit the ball gently. Try to keep it within the borders. If you do that again, we're going home."

He looked at the driving range. The tees were arranged in a slight arc facing an open field with several signs indicating the distance—from 100 to 300 yards—and several others sporting bull's-eyes. Several golfers on the far left of the ellipse were driving balls off wooden tees placed in the ground, but Mike and Watkins choose to drive from the rubber tees set on mats near the center of the arc. Mike selected first, so Watkins took the mat directly behind him.

He watched Mike's first shot, a powerful, high, deep shot that landed between the 200-and 250-yard markers. Watkins set his ball on the tee and gripped the club. He tried to recall the stance and swing he'd seen in the few seconds of golf he'd watched on Sunday afternoons as he flipped the stations during commercials. He swung, predictably leaving the ball unscathed. Another swing. A lot of air. A majestic swoosh. No contact. Another swing. Perhaps it was the wind, but this time the ball dribbled from the tee to a spot about five feet in front of the mat. Knowing the sport's reputation for decorum, Watkins wondered about driving range protocol. Should one attempt to retrieve the ball and return it to the tee, or did one leave it out there as a sign that one had no idea of what one was doing?

He got another ball from the basket and sent it to join the first. With an additional two balls in the cluster, Watkins began to feel deeply embarrassed and angry, and Mike's constant *whoosh–crack* wasn't helping matters. Watkins set a ball upon the tee. Rearing back and swinging for the 300-yard sign, he finally heard that satisfying sound of metal meeting dimpled plastic, but the ball, apparently with no regard for Watkins's intentions, took off in a sharply curved flight that carried it directly toward one of the real golfers teeing off from real tees on real grass.

*Jesus,* Watkins thought, *how'd I do that?* He looked over at the other golfer, who, though he was some distance away, Watkins could see was glaring at him. "Sorry!" Watkins yelled and set another ball on his tee.

"What happened?" Mike asked without looking.

"Nothing," Watkins replied, "just a wicked slice" *or hook—whatever the hell you call it.*

He stood over the ball, trembling but determined that this next swing would deliver the ball into territory yet unmeasured by yardage signs. He swung—hard. The ball, refusing to cooperate, remained defiantly in place. The club, however, its grip well oiled by the excessive sweat on Watkins's hands, sailed out over the range like a broken helicopter blade, and, following the same sickening curve taken by the only ball he'd made contact with, headed straight toward the real golfer.

"Look out! Look out!" Watkins yelled, jumping up and down.

"You don't have to say that on a driving range," Mike said, turning to look at Watkins just in time to see the club land safely a few yards from the other golfer, who screamed something Watkins couldn't completely make out because of the blood pounding in his ears. He was pretty sure, however, that he wasn't being invited to get his truck off the driving range.

Watkins bent down, picked up the bucket of balls, and walked to the concession. "I won't be needing these," he said handing the clerk the bucket.

"Where's the club?" she asked. With his thumb, he motioned over his shoulder. When he reached his car he yelled to Mike, who had apparently been watching him to this point, "See you tomorrow," saying it as if nothing out of the ordinary had occurred, as if on every Sunday morning he came to the driving range to throw a club at someone. He started his car and drove home.

At his apartment Watkins picked up the Sunday paper, which his elderly neighbor, Betty, had left, as she did every Sunday after she'd finished with it. He tossed it on the futon and opened his refrigerator to stare for a few moments at the three remaining beers, half jar of mayonnaise and dozen or so ketchup packets he'd pilfered from fast food restaurants. He got a glass of water from the tap, sat down and picked up the paper, which Betty had refolded with the sections misarranged. He rolled his eyes at the Sports section, which Betty had folded so that the story of Wexford's sorry performance in yesterday's game lay right on top. He flipped quickly past the classified and business sections, groaned as he flipped past the social section, and stopped, aghast, at the front page. He stood up, reading quickly past the headline and to the story:

# Student's Room Ransacked
*Washington Again Victim of Racism*

Responding to a call last night from James Washington, a first-year student living in Radar Hall on the campus of Wexford College, campus and local police discovered what looked like the set of a detective movie. The room was turned upside down, Treton City police officer Leslie Sanders told *The Call*. "Things were everywhere—clothes, books, papers, bedding, all over the place," Sanders said. "Drawers were pulled out of the dresser and the furniture was tipped over," she continued. "And the walls were covered with writing. On one wall, the 'N' word was written in huge, green letters."

In fact, the walls were reportedly covered with racial comments. One of the college administrators who saw the room claimed that green house paint had been used to write "N--- go home," and "Gorilla go back to the zoo" on several walls.

"Robbery does not seem to be the motive," according to investigating detective Janet Hobbs. According to Hobbs, nothing was missing from the dorm room, even though the room contained a stereo, a small television, compact music disks, and a number of other valuable items. "Whoever did this came here to send a message," Detective Hobbs said. "The racial comment is evidence enough of that."

Reached for comment late last night at the school's annual Parents' Weekend dinner party, Dean Matthews said that this is the worst racial incident to occur at Wexford since he became dean twenty years ago. "We will simply not tolerate this sort of behavior," he said. "When we find who did this, he will not be subjected merely to a disciplinary hearing. This is grounds for expulsion if we discover that this crime was committed by a student. I pray that it wasn't."

When asked if the case would be investigated by local authorities, Matthews said that the city police will notify state and federal authorities. "This is a clear cut violation of Mr. Washington's civil rights," claimed Matthews. "Whoever did this is in a great deal of trouble."

Earlier this semester, Mr. Washington was a victim of racial prejudice when another student at Wexford allegedly shoved him during a fight, called him a "gorilla," and accused "his people" of "wanting it all." That student faces a disciplinary hearing this Wednesday.

Several students gathered at the sight last night showed deep emotion over the incident. Dennis Shcherbak, a junior from Ukraine, told *The Call*, "This school has a reputation for tolerance and friendliness. I cannot believe that someone here would act this way. It is very depressing."

Deanna Richards, a senior, cried when she heard about the incident. "I hope they find who did this and lock him away," she said. "I'm thinking about going to another college next semester." Several other students commented that they felt a sense of hurt or anger.

James Washington is a first-year pre-med student from Springfield. He is also a starting wide-receiver for the Wexford Cardinals. He would not comment on the incident.

Watkins walked around his apartment rereading random portions of the article. *It can't be Tony*, he thought; *it can't be*. He'd come to believe Tony's explanation, and judging from how the furor had died down around campus, so had many of the other students. *But who?*

*Why?* he thought. Watkins felt sick in his stomach as he imagined Washington's reaction when he returned to his room. *The poor guy*, he thought. *He'll never stay here no*w.

Watkins was overcome with the desire to communicate with someone, but he didn't know anyone at work well enough to phone. He showered, changed and left his building, hoping to walk off some of the energy generated by the story. Outside his door, he met his neighbor.

"Oh, good morning, Betty. Thanks for the paper."

"Not such good news for the school there, Professor." She normally called Watkins "Peter" except when she was talking about the college, and most especially when she wanted to revel in the bad publicity the school sometimes suffered, such as when the police were called to break up loud parties or arrest underage drinkers or especially when one of the teams took another drubbing. "Can't anyone over there play a simple game of football?"

On a different day in a different place with a different person, Watkins would have been dismayed by the comment. But Betty was one of those gentle and friendly people who can so easily overlook the suffering and heartache of people not her own. "Betty," he said, "didn't you see the front page? A student's room was trashed and racist comments were written on the walls."

"Oh, yeah, I read the first few paragraphs. That kind of thing happens everyday. Vandals are everywhere. Not a thing you can do about it. Repaint the walls; they'll look good as new there."

Watkins thought for a moment about saying goodbye and leaving, but something inside him—the teacher or just the human being—forced him to stay and attempt a discussion. "Betty," he started, "it's not the walls that are damaged; it's the student, Jim Washington, who, you might know, plays for the football team."

"Is it the same guy?" she asked, evidently surprised. "Oh, he's a good one. Fast. They need more like him." Her passion for sports clearly exceeded her interest in social issues. "Don't you think? A few more guys who can catch the ball, and you might have something there. Oh, I remember when Wexford had the best team in the state. . . ." Watkins only half listened, astounded at Betty's memory for detail, but baffled by her refusal to discuss the incidents of the previous night. Finally, after she'd recounted almost every game of the 1956 championship season, Watkins asked her directly, "Betty, don't you think it's wrong to write, "Nigger, go home" on the wall of a black man's room?"

"Well, I would never do it. I can tell you that. But don't think that those same black men are so free from blame. Look at what happened in Woodtown the other week, with that black guy breakin' in and burnin' down that young family's home there. You know, what goes around comes around."

Watkins could see that Betty'd had enough of the conversation, but he tried once more: "Don't you think we should speak up against this sort of thing going on in our own town?"

"There's other things need speakin' out against, Professor, like how much money teachers get paid."

Watkins finally took the hint. "Thanks again for the paper, Betty," he said, returning, defeated, to his apartment, where he sat on the futon and turned on the television. He stared blankly at the screen for a few minutes before realizing that he was watching a football game. He flipped the channel. Golf.

### *John*

John awoke on Sunday morning after two fitful hours of sleep. His mind bubbled with thoughts. He tossed in bed for a few minutes and then sat up, resting his back against the wall. *I've gotta sort this out,* he thought. *My mother is in love with Eileen's father, so that'll make me her brother, which is okay since she thinks I'm a jerk anyway. Watkins knows I'm a jerk. And I know who destroyed Jim Washington's room. Now what?* Wanting to make sure that his mother got home safely, he got the phone from the desk and brought it to the bed.

"Hello."

"Hey, Mom. You got home okay," John said quietly.

"Oh, the road was so empty at midnight, it was no problem."

They talked for a few moments about how she could have stayed, but how she'd have felt awkward, and how it really wasn't difficult to drive the hour and a half home, and how next time she visited she'd get a hotel room, and they would have continued in that direction indefinitely, but John could restrain himself no longer.

"And besides, you wouldn't want your old mother hanging around on a Sun. . . . "

126

"Mom, are you in love with Mr. O'Neill?"

His mother didn't answer for a few seconds. "John, how could I be in love with him? We danced maybe four times. . . ."

"Seven."

"Okay, seven times. . . ."

"Four fast and three slow."

"Okay, I agree it was seven. . . ."

"And one was *extremely* slow."

"John!" she said, "one slow dance isn't slower than the others. I don't think. . . ."

"I meant closer."

"Well, he's a very warm and attractive man, honey, and I enjoyed his company very much. Now, I thought you were okay with this. You were so good about the last few dates I had."

John assured her that he didn't mind, really, that he wanted her to be happy, that he knew it was time for her move on with her life. "But," he added, "he lives too far away anyway."

"Well, now, honey, he's coming here next Saturday afternoon to take me to the East Mountain Arts Festival."

Silence.

"John? John, honey."

John stayed silent for a few moments more, not because he disapproved, but because he didn't want his mother to know that he was crying. Catching his breath, he cleared his throat and said, "That's great. It really is. You deserve to be happy. You've given me everything. You should get something back."

Silence.

"Mom? Mom?"

When she finally spoke, her words muffled and interrupted by sobs, she told John what he meant to her and how much she loved him. Then she added, "You know I'd like to give you a brother or sister while I'm still able to."

"You mean a sister like Eileen."

"Oh, that's right," she responded. "Well, you couldn't ask for a sweeter, more beautiful sister than her."

"I'm not picky. Feel free to find a man with less attractive children to be my siblings."

Joy laughed. "Hey, we're thinking way too far ahead here. I haven't even dated the man yet."

"Well, that one dance looked like a date to me."

His mother laughed. "Speaking of dancing, you should have danced with Eileen. I guess you really weren't feeling well, the way you left so early. You know you missed some commotion. I saw police cars on campus when I was leaving. And I came by to say goodnight, but you weren't in your room."

"I was in the bathroom."

"Oh, dear, you really were sick. Why didn't you tell me?"

"I, uh, I, um, I didn't want to ruin your night. I was okay. It was nothing."

Suddenly the conversation with Watkins occurred to John and simultaneously to his mother. "Oh, John, I hope I didn't embarrass you in front of your professor, but he caught me by surprise. I didn't know you told him your father was a policeman."

"That's okay, Ma. I'm sort of glad it came out. I was always nervous that he'd find out anyway. I know I shouldn't lie. In fact, I'm lying right now. I wasn't sick last night. Eileen makes me so nervous I had to get away from her. And when you came by I *was* in the bathroom, but I wasn't sick. I just had to go is all."

His mother clearly wanted to talk about his nervousness around Eileen, but John cut her off. "That isn't worrying me so much right now, Mom. I'll get over it. I actually have a more important problem right now."

"What?" his mother asked in her most concerned, maternal voice.

"Are you ready for this?" he asked, and continued without waiting for an answer. "I left you and the others at around 9:30, right? I went to my room and listened to music, read, watched television and just laid around. At about 11:30 I went to the bathroom."

John didn't go into any details about how it had taken him several months to get comfortable in a public bathroom, or how he preferred to schedule his visits during off-peak hours, except, of course, when he couldn't do anything about it, such as the few hours before one of those infuriating oral reports Professor Moss required in history class. No, his reasons for being in the bathroom at 11:30 weren't as important to the story as what happened there.

"So I'm, you know, in, you know, the stall," he said haltingly, embarrassed by the sudden realization that he was talking to his mother. "And anyway, the door opens. . . ."

"To the stall?!" his mother interrupted, sounding mortified.

"No, no, the main door, the bathroom door. And I hear these two voices. And one says to the other, 'Look at this. I carried this stupid thing all the way back here.' Then I heard something hit the garbage can. Then the other says, 'Man, we fixed that,' you know, 'nigger's ass.' Just like that, as if it were a KKK meeting or something. And the first guy says, 'This was perfect. We totaled that place. Maybe Washington'll get out now. Maybe they'll all get out.'"

"All who?" his mother asked.

"I guess all the black students," John replied. "There's some awful racism here, and there are only a few black guys. I could understand if they *do* leave after this."

"So what happened next?" his mother asked, obviously fascinated and probably nervous, John realized, that he somehow got involved and got hurt. She must have read his mind. "You didn't get hurt, did you?"

"No, they didn't know I was in there. I stayed perfectly still and silent. But I couldn't hear what they said next, because they turned on the water to clean their hands, I guess. When they were done, they left, and the last thing I heard was them laughing, and one says 'Hey, you better cover that up better,' and the other says, 'Dumb niggers. Let's see how fast they run now.'"

"What are you going to do?"

"I don't know," John responded.

"John?"

"Yes."

"Did you know them?"

He said nothing for a moment, and then, quietly, "Yes, one of them. He's in one of my classes. In fact, he lives here."

"Your roommate?" she asked, shocked.

John laughed. "Not quite," he said, thinking the question absurd. "Here—in the building."

"What are you going to do?" she repeated.

"I really don't know," John said. "I really don't know." They talked for a few minutes more. When he hung up, John got out of bed, pulled on a ratty sweatshirt and a pair of jeans, and sat back on the bed with his political science text book. He read a paragraph; then read it again. When he started it for the third time, he put the book down and stared straight ahead. *What am I going to do?* he thought.

He went to the desk, opened the bottom drawer and took out a bundle of industrial, brown paper towels. He unwrapped the bundle and was standing over it when the door flew open.

"Johnny Mariner, buddy. I'm baaaaack. How was the dance? D'ya get drunk with Mom? Hey what're ya doin' with that? Gonna paint the room? Good. It needs it. But that's a lousy color. Where's the can? Did you check. . . ."

"Nick."

"What?"

"You don't know what happened?"

"No, what happened?"

John told him.

"Who, John? Who did it? Tell me."

"I can't. I can't say right now."

"Why not? Because you know I'll kill him? Tell me, John. Was it Falcone? Tell me it was Falcone."

Nick's rage worried John. "I'll tell you when I figure out what I'm going to do," he replied.

Nick exploded. "Going to do? Going to do? What are you talking about? This is a no-brainer, John." He took a few steps toward John. "I saw Matthews walking toward the Student Center when I got back. I wondered why he was here on a Sunday. He's in his office. Go talk to him. Now, John!" he shouted. "Now!"

"Please, Nick, I need some time."

Nick grabbed the bundle. "I'll do it. I'll tell them it was Falcone."

"No, please Nick."

"Yeah, I'll tell them it was Falcone. Look at it this way: he'll be out of the picture, and you'll have a clear path to Eileen."

Although Nick clearly intended through his gesture and tone to ridicule him, John thought for a moment about this unforeseen upshot of letting Nick go to Matthews. *Falcone out of the picture. No! What am I thinking? That's insane. . . .* He shook his head as if to wake himself.

"Does that mean 'no'? Nick asked. "Does that mean, 'No, it wasn't Falcone,' or 'No, don't go to Matthews, I'll go'—meaning you, you'll go?"

"I meant no, I don't have to worry about Eileen anymore. Her father is in love with my mother and they'll probably get married, and Eileen will be my half-sister and you can't date your half-sister as far as I know."

Nick just stared at John for a few moments, and then stepped toward him, standing so close that John wondered it there was enough room in such a small space for John, Nick *and* Nick's chest. "John," Nick said slowly, "you really are one, first-class, certifiable lunatic. What kinda shit are you talking now?"

"My sister, I mean my mother is going to marry, I mean date Eileen's father. They met last night. They'll fall in love and get married. I know they will. You could just see it. You could sense it. I can't date Eileen—she'll be my half-sister."

"She'll be your step-sister, you doofus—if that. She might not be anything to you. And besides, you can still date her, marry her if you want. You're not related to her. You haven't lived with her as a sister all your life."

"Are you sure?"

"Yeah, I'm sure. Man, the things you worry about! Now what about Matthews? Are you going or am I?"

"You know what this is going to mean, Nick. I'll be in the paper. I'll probably have to testify at a disciplinary hearing. I might even have to testify at a trial. What if I'm wrong? What if I only think it's someone, but that person didn't do it?"

"You have the paintbrush. They'll get fingerprints."

"I need some time, Nick."

"You need more than time, John." Nick stood up and went to the door. "You remember what we talked about last week, John? About you're being so afraid? About needing to speak up? Well, here's your big moment. It's time to grow up." He walked out, shutting the door hard behind him.

"Nick!" John shouted after him, stepping toward the door but not opening it. He sat on the edge of the bed. *What* am *I afraid of now?* he wondered. *The attention? Getting beat up for snitching? Being labeled a squealer, a do-gooder, a geek? Looking like an administration spy? The praise? The press? The questions? The answers?* Did he not go immediately because he didn't think the crime was serious enough? No. He was disgusted, deeply offended by what he'd seen and heard. What was the problem? *Maybe Nick's right,* he thought. *I'm in a daze. I've been a spectator so long, I wouldn't know to duck a pitch coming straight at my head. I'm in a coma from staring straight ahead too long. Maybe,* he realized, *like everyone else, I've just gotten used to watching.* He remembered a time when he saw a father hold a child a foot off the ground by his wrist and slap him across the face for the unforgivable crime of jumping in puddles. No one came to that child's rescue. No one spoke up for that poor kid. No one moved, including him.

He'd listened a lot, read a lot, thought a lot in eighteen years of living in fear and obscurity, but for all his intelligence, his sensitivity, his imagination, he had learned only to think and sense, never to act. His only lesson was to live in a stupor, caught forever in that horrible moment of paralysis between knowing that something is terribly wrong and recognizing that something should be done. All that knowledge and no action. *Well*, he thought, *no more*. No more waiting to get struck in the temple with a screaming fastball. *It's time*, he thought and walked toward the door.

Having little practice, he wasn't sure how one actively participated in life. What are the procedures, the rules? He decided he'd have to learn as he went along. He knocked on Dean Matthews's office door.

"C'min"

John opened the door just enough to accommodate his head. "Dean Matthews?"

"Yes."

"I'm John Zajaczkiewicz. I'm a freshman."

"What can I do for you, John?"

"I know who destroyed Jim Washington's room."

Matthews stood up and walked immediately toward the door. "Come in, please, John. Come in."

# CHAPTER V

# Monday, December 1

*Hello, Eileen, this is John Zajaczkiewicz.* John sat at the desk in his room holding the telephone receiver on the base as if he expected it to jump off. In the other hand he held a piece of paper, reading it over and over, moving his lips as he went. The door slammed against the back of the chair.

"Oh, sorry, John. Since when do you use the desk?"

His stammering was sure to give him away. "I, uh, I needed to, um, uh. . . this is a serious phone call."

"One requiring a desk. I see," Nick responded teasingly. "What's that?"

"Just a piece of paper."

"If it's 'just a piece of paper,' then it must be important." In a blur, Nick grabbed the paper from John's hands.

"Jesus, Nick," John protested, annoyed that he hadn't anticipated Nick's quickness after being the victim of it all semester.

Nick read aloud. "Hello, Eileen, this is John Zah-what's his name. I'm calling to ask if you'll be kind enough to accompany me to the Spring Tip-off Dance on Saturday, January 17th. It would mean a lot to me." Nick's look said, "John, you poor, pitiful, simpleminded fool. It must be very painful being you." Before he could say all that out loud, John spoke up.

"C'mon, Nick, give me a break. I'm actually willing to learn how to dance for this. But I've never called a girl. Well, I mean, I've never actually waited until someone picked up the phone before. I'll choke. I'll forget why I called. I'll make an idiot of myself."

"Yeah, I guess making an idiot of yourself wouldn't be as bad as calling and reading a prepared text that contains the phrase 'kind enough to accompany me.' Yeah, that's a much better idea. You'll seem perfectly normal to her that way. Pure genius, John. How do you do it? Man, I just do not understand you. You've sat beside her for over a month in class, you've met her in the library, you see her all the time. She was at your house with the whole family for Thanksgiving dinner. Why don't you just ask her out?"

"I *am* asking her out. I'm not sure *how* to ask her out. She's going to know I've never done this before. She's going to give me that 'Let's not ruin our friendship' line. She's going to be embarrassed I even asked. She's. . . ."

"Okay, here's what you do." Nick demonstrated his technique for John, swaggering toward the desk, leaning on it as if it were a very low bar in a dimly lit lounge, asking John in his best baritone what a nice guy like him was doing in a dorm room like this.

"You're scaring me, Nick."

Nick laughed and grabbed John's entire face between his thumb and the rest of his huge hand until John's lips puckered. Nick leaned toward John.

"On ew air ish e," John said.

Without letting go, Nick relaxed his grasp. "Huh, John, what was that?"

"Don't you dare kiss me."

Nick's laughter could probably be heard throughout the building. It was the deep, muscular laugh of a powerful and happy man. "I *should* kiss you, Johnny Mariner. You know you're my favorite person in the whole world." He released John's face and took a framed newspaper article from the wall. "Student arrested in racial incident," he read. "Falcone cleared of all charges. Campus Police today released the name of the student arrested on Monday for the racially motivated vandalism of James Washington's dorm room. Acting on a tip from another student, police arrested Robert Henderson, a first-year student from Woodtown, and charged him with eight separate accounts. . . ." Nick had crossed out some of the paragraph and had added in red ink, "Acting on a tip from my roomie, John Mariner Z-man, police arrested the asshole Robert Henderson." He never tired of reading the paragraph, sometimes with the revision, aloud to John.

"You da man, John. You zee man. You John zee man."

"Please don't start that; it'll stick. Help me with this. What do I say to Eileen?"

"First of all, don't call her. Ask her when you see her, face to face. The phone's too impersonal. Ask her in Watkins's class."

"What if I have a heart attack?"

"Hey, she'll have to resuscitate you. Although with your luck, Watkins will do it, and when you wake up staring into his face you'll have another heart attack, and the cycle will continue for the entire seventy-five minute period. Better tell Watkins your plans before class just in case."

John gave Nick a withering look. "Please."

Nick and John talked for half an hour on the various approaches to the terrifying—for John—act of asking a woman on a date. Finally, Nick said, "Look, John, here's a novel idea: be yourself. If she likes who you are, she'll say yes. If she says no, settle for a really frustrating brother-sister relationship. But I have a feeling she's not saying no."

"I don't think being myself is going to work. I think I need a new self. I'm going to dress all in black, carry a beeper and a cell phone, smoke cigars, get highlights in my hair, pierth my tongue, grow a goatee, wear polyester, drink cappuccino, quote Tarantino. Hey, we could redo the room, put up Marilyn Monroe and Charlie Parker posters, have Christmas lights all year, get a lava lamp and a wine rack." John acted out each possibility, stroking his chin, smoking a non-existent cigar, sipping from a non-existent cup, walking like a model, prancing around the room and indicating with exaggerated motions where the posters and lava lamp would go.

"Wow, look at how fast the time went," Nick said checking his watch. "Visiting hours are over already. I'll see you tomorrow. Can I bring you anything?" He picked up John's script from the desktop and tore it in half. "Be yourself, you lunatic. You don't look good in black."

John could hear Nick's laughter outside the door. *He's right*, he thought. *It's not as if we never met. It's not as if we didn't sit right beside each other at dinner. It's not as if I didn't say "Yes, I'd like a piece of turkey" and then say "chest" because I couldn't get out the word "breast" and it didn't occur to me to say "white" when she asked me which part.* John cringed at the memory and then smiled recalling everyone's reaction. Eileen just looked confused. "Chest?" she asked; "Is that different from the breast?" The entire table had gone into hysterics. Her father almost choked laughing. Even Maury got in on the act, holding up various pieces of meat during the meal and asking, "What do you call this, John?" Eileen's grandmother made some weak effort to defend John by comparing him to her own Victorian grandparents, and then deflated

John's hopes of a reprieve by following her defense with a request to pass her a "lower appendage."

He recalled their laughter—and his own. He'd been the cause of the hilarity, but the ribbing he took was so good natured and affectionate that he felt only complimented and encouraged by it. It wasn't derisive or cruel. There was reason to laugh, and he knew it. He had started to laugh with them, and the memory now caused him to chuckle.

The laughter in his mind blended with the faint sound of Nick's in the hall. There was something in that moment—the memory and the reality of laughter—that changed John forever. He opened his English notebook and dialed the phone.

"Hello."

"Hello, Professor Watkins. This is John Zajaczkiewicz. I'm in your writing class. I'm sorry to call you at home."

"That's okay, John. That's why I put my number on the syllabus. What's up? Is something wrong?"

"No, nothing's wrong. I was just wondering if I might be able to see you after class tomorrow. I want to ask you about something."

"No problem at all. I'll see you in my office right after class. Are you sure you're okay?"

John swore he was fine and said goodbye.


### Watkins

With the pen in his right hand, Watkins slapped his left hand palm down, fingers spread upon the sheet of paper he'd just written on, crumpled it in his fist and tossed it on the floor. He started again: "Dear Diane, I just received your latest postcard—another one of those damned stupid ridiculous meaningless infuriating bullshit postcards." Slap, crumple, toss. "Dear Diane, You heartless mean, cruel . . . " Slap, crumple, toss. "Dear Diane, Or should I say Diane and Ridge? I still can't get over that! Why don't you just tear my heart out. . . ." Slap, crumble. The phone rang. After his short conversation with John Zajaczkiewicz, Watkins returned to the stack of blank sheets on his desk. He reread Diane's latest postcard:

Peter—
The end is in sight! I have a defense date and have sent out a thousand applications—some of them are near where you're teaching. Maybe we'll be neighbors. Wish me luck. Diane.

He laid the postcard on the desk and looked at the last false start, still lying half crushed on top of the stack of clean sheets. His eyes fell on "my heart," and he read it out loud several times, then picked up his pen and started again: Dear Diane, I love you. I have loved you since I took the seat next to yours in our first class together, but I could never find the strength or courage to tell you. And now it is too late." He wrote a dozen pages, front and back, filled with memories, confessions, humor and heartache. He interpreted every action that had either confused her or left no impression: "Remember how by sheer coincidence I just happened to reserve the carrel in the library right next to yours? That coincidence cost me $100 to the guy who originally had it." And "wasn't it odd how we always happened to be parking at just about the same moment—just before 8:00 in the morning—even though *my* classes started at noon? You loved those morning classes. I had to have three alarm clocks. Did you really think I used all that time to prepare? I slept in my office."

Without pausing, he wrote until the last paragraph: "Diane, I'm sorry about all this—this mess of writing telling you about my feelings. I've probably embarrassed you. If I never hear from you again, I'll know why. Love, Peter."

He folded the letter, and tried to stuff it into an envelope too small for so many pages. With the help of some ugly creases, he managed to seal the flap, and he attached six stamps just to be sure that the post office wouldn't refuse to mail the unwieldy bundle. Normally he would have spent days tossing around the decision of whether to send such a letter, deciding with conviction one way and then the other. But tonight, as if to prevent any vacillation, he walked quickly to the mailbox. Returning to his apartment exhausted, he went to bed at 9:00.

# Tuesday, December 2

## *Watkins*

Unable to sleep longer, he arose at 5:00. His final dream of the night, the one he most remembered, had him running through a storm of golf balls as he desperately tried to reach a post office that was about to close. He arrived just as the door was being locked by Ridge Rowlands, and when he looked into his hand at what he was attempting to mail, he found his dissertation, reduced to two hand-written pages and stamped just above the title with a Mr. Yuk sticker like the ones his mother used to put on cleaning fluids and medicines. When Watkins awoke, he marveled at how many of his anxieties managed to find space in a single dream.

He used the four hours before class to shower, straighten his apartment and read over his notes. With only one week remaining in the semester, he figured that if he hoped to teach his students anything at all about writing, he had only two days in which to do so, but because he had to distribute evaluations and take care of other matters on the last day, he really had only one.

At 9:00 he started class and for the next 75 minutes presented a good three weeks worth of material to his students so that most of them were in a complete trance by about 9:02. At 10:15 he dismissed them, and as they filed like zombies past his desk, Watkins stopped John. "I'll see you in few minutes, right, John?" he asked.

"Huh, oh yeah, okay, see you in few minutes," John replied and shuffled out with the others.

Watkins left the classroom just as two of his colleagues appeared in the hall. Together they began the climb up the stairs to their offices, complaining as they went about how quickly the semester seemed to pass. Suddenly someone going down grabbed his shirt. He stopped and looked into the face of Walter Golden, an ancient, highly regarded member of the faculty, a full professor of philosophy for the past thirty years, a man of supremely even temperament and complex thoughts, a graceful man who charmed every member of the faculty and bored to tears every one of his students.

"There was a student in my class today spitting tobacco juice in a soda bottle," Golden said staring at Watkins. "Spitting in a bottle! I wasn't imagining it. I can't take much more, Peter. I mean, they sit there with their baseball caps pulled down over their eyes, their feet up on the chair in front of them, looking smug and disinterested, as if they're daring me to teach them something. They're all so apathetic and bored, with their 'done there, been that' attitude. I had a student in class this morning with those headphones on, that watchamacallit, the Sony Man. Sitting there—while I'm talking—with headphones on! The nerve."

Golden kept a tight grip on Watkins's shirt sleeve, so that if Watkins had wanted to move he couldn't. "They make no effort to stifle their yawning; I can see their dental work half the time. They wear their pants so I can see their underwear. Some of them sleep in class. They're taking $20,000 naps, for Christ's sake. I'm starting to wonder how much longer I can take it. Don't they realize I'm up there trying to do my job? I'm not here for me. What's wrong with these kids? Tell me, Watkins, what's wrong?"

He seemed sad and frustrated, not angry. To Watkins, Golden was truly bewildered, and not because he missed the days of thin ties, crew cuts, madras and khaki, the days when men removed their hats in buildings, addressed their professors as "Sir," and were the only gender in the classroom. Golden was the kind of professor who adapted easily to the shifts of fashion and decorum. The loss of a dress code didn't bother him. He wasn't longing for the days of authority and mind-numbing discipline. It was the simple lack of *all* courtesy that bothered him and the apparent disdain with which his students considered their education and perhaps their educators. He was taking it personally, and after years of trying to solve the puzzle of youth, he was apparently turning to Watkins for some insight. Not even a dozen years beyond adolescence himself, maybe Watkins had some answers.

*It's "been there, done that,"* he thought of saying. Then, *they're young; they're supposed to act that way. They're doing exactly what we expect them to do.*

*Maybe they're doing it to annoy you* occurred to him as a response, but he rejected it also. "I don't know, Walt," he said. "Have you asked them?"

141

"Asked them what? Why they act the way they do? Do *they* know why they act the way they do? Ask them! You're not helping me here, Peter."

*You're not on the tenure committee by any chance, are you?*—another impulse Watkins wisely resisted.

"Maybe you could work your feelings into a lesson. Is there anywhere in your courses where you might fit a discussion on the behaviors or attitudes of youth? Maybe a philosophical approach?"

"Ha! Okay, Peter, I'll tell them how Socrates' students spit tobacco juice and wore their laurels backwards."

"Well, some of them might have," Watkins returned, laughing softly in the hope Golden would do the same. "Maybe the hedonists, you know."

"You're no help, Peter." Golden released Watkins's sleeve and continued down the stairs, stopping after a few steps and turning toward Watkins. "You'll find out, though. After a few years, you get tired of the attitude. They're supposed to be here to learn something, not show off what they think they know." He disappeared down the staircase. Golden was probably right about one thing: although Watkins had noticed in his own students much of what the older professor had seen, Watkins was not yet troubled by it. Maybe it was his youth, or perhaps he was concerned with other matters, such as surviving each day in the classroom. The luxury of analyzing student behavior probably came with tenure, but Watkins was more concerned with making the right impression on everyone. He thought about the course evaluations he had to distribute in a few days. *I hope they know I've tried to do my job, too, Walt,* he thought.

Watkins had no sooner shut the door to his office when he heard a knock. He invited John to sit. "How's everything, John? How's your mom?"

"Oh, she's fine, thanks. She's looking forward to another school function. She didn't get a chance to dance to 'Louie, Louie,' so her night was incomplete."

Watkins laughed. "Well," he said, "she sure can dance."

"She lives for it. She dances all over the house sometimes." Watkins had no problem with that image. "It's like something inside her just gets her moving. Sometimes I think she dances without realizing she's doing it."

"It must be great to be so free and so un-self-conscious," Watkins said.

"Yeah, I wouldn't know."

"Me neither," Watkins replied.

"What?"

Watkins realized what he'd said. "Oh, I mean I don't like to dance either. So what's on your mind, John?"

"Do you remember when we had that talk about a month ago, after Parents' Weekend, when I told you, well, when you found out, that my father left us and I made up having one? Well, remember how you told me that I shouldn't make up stories in essays, but that I might look into creative writing. I've decided to take your advice. I want to become an English major and register for the short story writing class next semester. I think I want to be a writer."

"Hey! Terrific, John. My first recruit. What made you so sure?"

"I don't know. All my life I avoided getting involved in anything that would attract attention because I didn't want anyone laughing at me or thinking I was dumb. I made up stories about my family"—he paused and grinned at Watkins—"Oh, yeah, you know that. Well I think I did that to keep people from knowing the truth about me because I thought no one would care to know me. And then I started to hate people just so I wouldn't have to deal with them. Well not actually hate them, you know. More like afraid of them. I was just like"—he scrunched up his face and rocked his head as if to shake the right words loose.

### John

*Serious.* "I was so serious all the time." In the fraction of a second John needed to catch his breath, he suddenly felt embarrassed. *He must think I'm a lunatic. I've hardly said a word to him all year, and now I can't shut up.* Instantly he heard Nick's voice, *Be yourself, you lunatic.* "I've learned a lot here, not so much from the books, but from being with people. I really like my roommate and some of the kids in our class and Eileen's family and you."

Watkins looked startled. "I mean, you know . . . you know what I mean, I um. . . ."

"I know what you mean, John. Thanks."

"I'm still not sure of who I am because I've avoided finding out, but I know that I want to find out, and I'm not so afraid of finding out and I'm not so afraid of letting people know me. *Did I say "find" enough? Be yourself, you lunatic.* You always say writing is a way to discover who we are and get involved in the world at the same time. Well, I want to tell people who I am and make them laugh and think and cry. I want to be a writer. I'm not sure I can do it, but it's what I want to do. My roommate told me that I was letting life pass me by, and I think he was right. But it's not life itself, it's, I don't know, it's, like, life-in-life. Do you know what I mean? *You're ranting.* I'm ranting. *You should just shut up.* I should just shut up."

"No, no," Watkins insisted, "go on. Please, go on."

"It's the joy of life I miss, the being with people, you know, the happiness. I'm still not going to be a tennis player or try out for a part in a school play. I'm still nervous about a lot of things. I'm not making sense."

"Yes, you are."

"I want to make more friends, go to parties, maybe even join a club—something low key. Is there a low key club?"

Watkins laughed. "You mean you're not ready for the cheerleading squad?"

"Maybe next semester. I don't know, I just feel like I want to find out what life is like out there. A lot has happened to me this semester. I think I grew up more in two months than I did in the eighteen years before that. I think the thing I found out most is— *you lunatic*—even if I'm a nut case, there are people out there who like me anyway." Watkins sat quietly, smiling and nodding gently. In the moment of silence John noticed that he and Watkins were sitting the same way, one ankle on the opposite knee, both hands holding their shins. It occurred to John that he was looking at his future. He reached for his cap.

### Watkins

As John talked, Watkins watched him twist and fidget in the chair, place one leg across the other, shake his foot and tug at his cap. Finally, John placed his palm on top of the cap and pushed it back on his head so that the bill was completely off his face. John's candor had stunned him somewhat. Never before had he seen such spirit and hope in a young man. Well, maybe once before.

"Okay, you madman," he said smiling, "it's decided. I'll have to check with the department chair and the professor who teaches short story writing to see if I can register you for the class. It's an upper division course, and you're a first-year student, but, then again, your grade in writing is good enough that I could probably argue to have you registered."

"How good?"

"Pardon me?"

"How good is my grade in writing?"

Watkins was astounded. "I can't believe you're asking me that question, John. After all you've just said. Oh, wait, I get it. I'm supposed to laugh."

"Uh, not really."

"John! After everything else, you're still worried about grades!"

"Not all of them. I let everything else slip a little after Parents' Weekend. But, yeah, I guess I still do worry about the grade. Maybe I do worry a bit too much about the final evaluation—being told I did okay. Is that so bad?"

Watkins looked at John. *Were you reading my mind coming up the stairs? Did I leave a trail of thoughts behind me?* he wanted to ask. He smiled and said instead, "No, it's not."

"Do I have a chance at an A? Did you notice that I got A's on my last two papers?"

"Yes, John, I noticed. And, yes, you have a chance at an A. Now get out of here before I change my mind."

John stood to leave. "Thanks, Professor. Thanks for everything."

"My pleasure, John." John opened the door. "Oh, John?"

"Yes."

"Uh . . . nothing. Thanks. I'll see you Thursday."

# Thursday, December 4

### Eileen

Eileen arrived to her last writing class ten minutes early and took the seat she'd been sitting in since the middle of the semester—last row, second seat from the left-hand corner, right next to John Zajaczkiewicz. She was happy to have found such a close friend, a surrogate brother, and she enjoyed talking to John about their parents. Her father seemed to be getting more and more comfortable with the idea of falling in love again. Maury would not heal for many years or maybe forever, but Eileen saw glimpses of joy even in her. As Eileen sat waiting for class to begin, it occurred to her that she would miss it.

"Eileen, you're here early."

"Hi, John. I'm not sure why I got here so soon. I guess I just wanted to get a long last look at the room. This room means a lot to me now." She wondered if John would have any idea of what she meant.

### John

John had no idea of what she meant. In fact, he couldn't really hear what she was saying because of the squeaky and persistent voice that repeated again and again, "Eileen, willyougowithmetotheSpringTip-offDanceinthespringpleasepleaseplease? Eileen, willyougowithmetotheSpringTip-offDanceinthespringpleeeeeeeeeeease pleasepleasepleaseEileen?" And a slightly deeper voice that responded *The Spring Tip-off Dance in the spring! When else would it be, you idiot? Oh this is good. Real good, John.* Meanwhile, Eileen's lips continued to move.

"Well, this is it!" he heard, finally breaking up the dialogue in his head, but it didn't come from Eileen.

"Well, this is it," Watkins said as he opened the door of room 312 for the last time of the fall semester. "We made it. I have just a few things to do today, so I'll get started right away." For about twenty minutes he talked about writing in other disciplines and about taking essay tests in college, being careful all the while to present a manageable amount of information. At the end of the lesson he removed the evaluation forms from a manila envelope and distributed them, wishing that he could treat them lightly, but too nervous to say or do anything but leave the room as the students filled in bubbles that could alter the course of his life. He knew that no matter what the results, he would misinterpret them. If they enjoyed the class, he'd convince himself that he had tried too hard to avoid offending and that he'd been too entertaining, pandering to their desire to be complimented and amused. If one student found him humorless or unfair, he'd ignore the eighteen who found him bearable or challenging. He returned after a few minutes and asked Theodore to collect the evaluations, seal them in the manila envelope addressed to the department chair and drop them in campus mail.

"I'm glad to be able to do this for you, Professor," Theodore said, licking the envelope and pressing the flap to seal it. "I mean take this envelope straight to the campus post office and all. Guarding it with my life so that no one tries to grab it away and change all the scores to zeros or anything like that. It's my pleasure to help out. Oh, by the way. . . ."

"Can it, Teddy," Pete Churnip said.

"Thank you, Pete," Watkins said. "Keep an eye on him for me, will ya?" Pete leaned across the aisle and set his face on Theodore's shoulder.

"Very funny. Everyone's in a good mood, apparently. Is that a good sign or a bad sign, I wonder? By the way, I did tell you all how much I've enjoyed this class and how wonderful you've all been, didn't I?"

"Too late," Theodore said waving the envelope and smiling. Watkins laughed. Hesitating for a moment, he decided to continue.

"I hate to shatter the levity, but something happened to me after class on Tuesday that I want to share with you." Without mentioning the name, he told them about Golden. He couldn't remember all the details of Golden's lament, but he remembered several and he caught the essence. "I'm afraid that he's not alone," Watkins concluded. "Your generation often gets attacked by others with similar complaints. I'm not telling you this to upset you at the end of the semester, though I wisely, you might notice, let you evaluate the class first. I really want to know how you feel. The times seem to be changing very quickly; some of your professors might be having trouble keeping up."

No one said a word. Pete, Belinda, Ann Marie, Meagan, Theodore, Christian, Eileen, Jessica—all of the students Watkins had come to depend on during the semester sat quietly, some staring straight ahead, some looking at their notebooks or empty desks. Watkins wondered for a moment if he'd made an awful mistake—the last day of class and he was leaving them feeling defeated and chastened. He'd hoped for rousing indignation. Now he felt his only hope was to answer the question himself—"I, uh, I'm not sure I would, uh . . ."—but he was interrupted.

"He's generalizing."

A great sense of relief came over Watkins as he scanned the class for the unfamiliar source of the comment. "Someone wanted to say something? I didn't quite hear what was said. Did someone back there want to make a point?"


### *John*


*Oh my God! Was that my voice? Did I say that?* Judging from the look on Eileen's face and the fact that several students had turned to look at him, John concluded that, indeed, the voice had come from him and, prepared or not, he had better finish the thought—out loud.

"I think the professor you mentioned is generalizing. Some people are like that. But, I mean, maybe he's concentrating too much on the negative and not enough on what's really great about this generation. (*Where is this coming from?*) It's like how you remember insults more than compliments, or how when you get a paper back (*geez, I'm on a roll here*) and it's all marked up and you think 'how could I have made those mistakes?' instead of saying, 'oh, I'm glad I did this part or that part correctly.' I think there are some terrific people here. Maybe you just have to focus on them."

When Jen turned around to smile at him, he noticed several other students looking his way, some of them with approving looks, others maybe just curious to see who the new guy was. Watkins, too, was smiling.

"He's right," Ann Marie added. "There's assholes, sorry, idiots in every generation, and I'm sure there are plenty in mine, but not all of us are that way. I usually spit my tobacco juice out the window."

"That's you?!" Pete said.

"I also think that guy's right, Belinda said nodding toward John. *Wait a minute,* John thought, *we met,* and then remembered that it had been in the first week of class. She had apparently forgotten his name. "You know, it's, like, when you give a speech in speech class, and, you know, like, this one guy's rollin' his eyes and you think, like, what's wrong? Why don't you like my speech, you know? And then, like, everyone after class says, like, 'Oh, I liked your speech,' but all you think about is, like, that one guy. You know what I mean?"

"I have a vague notion," Watkins replied.

"It's true that we tend to pay too much attention to the odd ball in the group, but maybe that's why some people act that way, for the attention," Pete Churnip added. "Everyone's looking for a way to stand out in the crowd, to be cooler than the rest. Ironically, we usually try to be cool in the most fashionable way."

"That's it," Jessica said excitedly, "and for some reason, a lot of young people think that the coolest way to act is to pretend they are completely unaffected by anything. They're bored because they've seen and done it all at eighteen and there's no excitement left."

"Yeah," someone added, "that's why you hear that 'been there, done that' comment all the time? or 'whatever'? It's cool to be bored?" He wasn't asking questions. That's just the way he spoke.

"I hate that expression," Theodore said. "Hey, how come no one ever says it about sex? 'Oh, no thank you. Been there, done that'?"

When the laughing stopped, Pete Churnip spoke. "Everyone knows that's just a defense mechanism. "They're just covering for inadequacies. No one really takes that "been there, done that" stuff seriously, except to sell soda or sneakers."

"Defense mechanism? Inadequacies? Looks like someone's passing Psychology this semester," a dismayed Gary Kardell added.

"Yes!" Jessica replied quickly. "It is just a defense, but somehow people really seem to believe that attitude substitutes for intelligence these days. You don't have to know anything; just pretend that you do and that you're above repeating it or discussing it."

"Well, what about John's original point?" Watkins asked looking at his watch. "What about what's good with your generation?"

"We don't have enough time to discuss that," Jen said.

"Well, with a few obvious exceptions," Jessica said glancing in the direction of Robert Henderson's empty chair, "I think this generation can be very friendly and tolerant. People still assume a lot of things about me because I look Asian, and sometimes I get insulted, but most people my age have been very nice to me and have made me feel very welcomed."

"We haven't forgotten that there's a lot of racism and hatred and violence in the world," Jen said.

"Yeah," Belinda agreed, "a lot of, like, drugs and crime."

"And poverty," someone added.

"And divorce."

"And lonely children."

"That's true," Jessica continued. "Most of us know what's out there, and some of us have a lot of sadness in our own lives. But, even with all that, I think that we recognize diversity more than any generation before us. We're used to living among different people. It's really no big deal."

"I don't know," Pete interrupted. "There's still so much racism and segregation around. Look at television. You have white shows and black shows. Music is segregated. The Internet gives every racist lunatic with a computer a chance to spread his disease. Every crack baby is black in the media. Cops suspect blacks first. More blacks on death row. I don't think things are as good as you make them sound. Look in this room!"

"I agree," Jessica returned, "but I'm talking about a one-on-one level. Individuals can overcome their prejudices. You have to start somewhere, and maybe our generation is the place to start.. At least *we're* willing to talk about it. At least we're willing to act. Look at the kid who turned Henderson in."

150

No one did of course. Only Nick and Jen knew what John had done, and that's the way he wanted it. He wasn't ready for *that* much attention.

Peter assented slightly. "I suppose you're right. It's a racist culture and hatred is everywhere. But I guess things will change a bit if people our age do something about their inherited racism. Of course some of us just genuinely try to be kind, and that's okay, too." He looked at Ann Marie.

"Don't start on me," she said.

"It was a compliment!" They both laughed

"Ann Marie said it," Jessica added. "The people who still unfairly judge others or exclude people because of their race, well, she called them what they are. The rest of us, I think need to count on each other for respect and support. I think we can be there for each other."

"I hope you are," Watkins said. "Well, everyone," he continued after checking his watch, "I think Jessica's comments might stand as the last word on the semester. Thank you all for an enjoyable and rewarding fifteen weeks. Remember, there's no final in this writing class. I'll have your grades calculated and posted on my door sometime early next week. Let's say by Monday."

"So we should come by Thursday or Friday?" Theodore Crossings asked.

"At the earliest," Watkins replied, grinning. "Thanks again, everyone. Good luck to all of you. See you in the spring."

*Spring!* John's thoughts boiled and a few words rose here and there to the top: *spring, dance, Eileen, dance, damn, spring, Eileen.*

Eileen turned to him. "I'm sorry to see it end."

"What?"

"The course?" she replied, looking confused.

"Oh, yeah. Me, too. Eileen, will you please . . . let me walk you to your car?"

"Great," she replied. "Let me just say goodbye to Tony."

With only the slightest twinge of jealousy, John watched her kiss Tony's cheek. What he mostly felt was a profound respect for her kind-heartedness, an intense attraction for her beauty, a fierce love, and an overwhelming desire to throw up. He thought for a moment about leaving, but instead he walked toward Watkins.

"John!" It was Jen. "I'll see you later. Oh, I liked what you said in class—about looking at the positive."

"Well, I owe a lot of those feelings to Nick, you know. I don't know what I would have done without him."

"Speaking of Nick, I'm telling my parents tonight. Wish me luck."

John did and approached Watkins. "Thanks again, Professor. I enjoyed the class very much. I guess I'll be seeing you for other classes in the future."

"I hope so, John. And thank you for getting things started here today. I appreciated that very much."

"Enough for an A?"

"My God, you're impossible."

"I'm just joking." He paused. "Sort of."

"I'm ready, John," Eileen said. "Thanks, Professor."

"My pleasure, Eileen."

With Eileen beside him and Watkins a few steps behind, John walked out of room 312.


### Watkins

*What did I expect?* Watkins wondered as he waited fearfully for his students to defend themselves. Despite what he said, he *had* told them about Golden's comment because he wanted to anger them, to challenge them, to goad them into a passionate defense of themselves. He wanted to see someone pound the desk in an inspired refutation of Golden's evaluation. He had done it to let them know what others knew—that the coolness was transparent, that attitude was not an accomplishment. He expected indignation, and it hadn't occurred to him that, met with silence, he'd have to apologize or defend them himself to avoid saying goodbye in misery. In those few unbearable seconds of silence, wondering if he'd made a mistake, Watkins considered for a brief moment that Golden may have been right; maybe they were too bored to bother. Where was their passion?

And then someone spoke. And then the rest. Were they right? Did their tolerance of one another save them? Were they the last best hope to end prejudice and repression, or did they accept one another primarily because they just didn't care? Had they indeed learned so well not to confuse difference with inferiority, taken so seriously the warnings against judging others, that they had truly come to respect one another, or were they merely flocking together—anonymous, indifferent and safe? Was it complacency masquerading as tolerance, or had they learned the lessons of communion, compassion and clemency?

"Love one another."

"Whatever."

He wasn't sure.

Maybe Jessica knew better. Maybe she was right; maybe they'd be there for each other? Some, maybe. He watched them walk from his class, knowing that whatever he might say about any one of them he couldn't say about all of them. Individually they would accept and reject, include and exclude one another, appreciate difference and yield to their prejudices. They would harbor resentment and animosity, act cruelly, refuse to forgive, seek revenge, plot retributions. They would commit acts of limitless generosity, pardon and absolve, console and encourage one another. They would be brothers and sisters, enemies and allies. They'd fall in and out of love, break each other's hearts, find themselves and lose themselves. They would struggle, falter, rise or fall, and they would discover lives of joy and sadness, hope and despair, and find in every new day some fresh challenge for their hearts and minds.

It wasn't easy saying goodbye, he realized, especially to young people whose lives lay ahead of them. How many of them would attain Pete's awareness or Jessica's insight (or the courage of either) or Ann Marie's sensitivity or Theodore's humor? Would they find inspiration, act passionately, live fiercely? Would they learn to dance every day to the extraordinary music of their young lives? Would they be happy? *I hope you are.*

Having said goodbye to John and Eileen, Watkins collected his things and walked down the hall a few steps behind them. As his two former students turned toward the stairs, he listened to their conversation.

"I'm parked right outside the building for once. Do you believe it? On the last day."

"Is your muffler still broken?"

"Unless someone found it and did something about it. It fell off yesterday. My father swore he'd fix it today. I can't tell you how embarrassing it is to drive around like that."

"Now I'll bet *everyone's* looking at you." Watkins understood, but she didn't.

"That's what I mean," she said.

As they entered the stairway, Eileen and John started down; Watkins started up.

"Eileen," he heard John say, "I was wondering if I could ask you something."

"What is it, John?"

*Yeah, John, what is it?* Watkins was too far away to hear the rest.

### Eileen

As Eileen pulled away from the curb, she turned the radio up. The caller wanted advice on her relationship with an alcoholic. By way of an answer, the doctor provided a comparison: "I don't understand why women settle in their relationships for guys that have problems. You know how birds mate? A female bird will look around for the best mate she kind find, and if she's with one male bird and some other male bird has a better plumage or builds a better nest, she'll drop the first mate and go to the other, the better one." The caller's reluctance to leave a man she deeply loved apparently struck Sally as hilarious, and she laughed aggressively.

"Good bye forever, Doctor!" Eileen said. She punched the first button on the radio. "Here's the Kingsmen with a song that's over thirty years old. Can you believe it? Thirty years! Your parents danced to this one. Sing along, if you can figure out the words." Eileen cranked the volume as loud as it would go and sang along as best she could.

When she got home, she found her grandmother in the usual spot. "Hi, Nana, I'm home."

"I know. I had three blocks' advanced notice."

"Dad said he'd fix it tonight."

"Oh, he called. He said take it down to Bill's. He'll fix it. You're father's going to repair his porch in exchange."

"Great. I'll go this afternoon."

"I was wondering if you'd want to clean the downstairs this morning, Eileen."

"Let's not, Nana. It really doesn't need it. I want you to tell me more about you and Granddad. How'd you meet? What was he like when he was young? How did you know when you were in love?"

"Oh, you should have known him when he was young. He was sooo handsome." She placed her hand over her heart. "Everyone said so. . . ."

Eileen turned off the television, and they talked for hours.

# *Saturday, December 6*

"Are you writing these down, Petey?"

"Yes, Mom. Lord and Taylor's, Eddie Bauer and Macy's. I have them. Are you sure this is what they want?"

"Of course it is. They look forward every year to your gift certificates. Don't go disappointing them and buying gifts. They'll never forgive you for making them stand in the exchange lines." They talked for a few minutes more, until Mrs. Watkins apparently picked up her son's signals. "Am I keeping you from something, Petey?"

He explained that he was overwhelmed with work and that grades were due shortly. "I'll call you tomorrow," Watkins said and returned to the television to see if the Celtics had scored in the fifteen minutes he'd been away. His newly discovered love of basketball was due primarily to the stack of essays awaiting him. When the game ended, he tried valiantly to enjoy the men's figure skating championships that followed, but he finally surrendered to the essays. To remind himself of what he'd be looking for, he reread the assignment:

> **Paper 6:** Over the course of the semester, you've written papers about yourself, your family, your generation, a problem confronting your nation and a issue of historical or international importance. You've written over three thousand words primarily because I made you do it. So now let me ask you a question: Why write? Why bother to put yourselves through the agony of finding topics, gathering ideas, organizing and drafting, revising and editing? What's the use? Was it all just for a grade?

The assignment continued for a few more paragraphs, in which Watkins cautioned his students against flattering him or evaluating the course. "More than anything else," he wrote, "I want to know why anyone should bother writing."

Among the essays were the usual assortment of disappointments, just-so compositions and spectacular creations listing a variety of reasons for putting pen to paper: "to express my ideas," "to write better essay exams and improve my grades," "to be more successful in college and in my job," "to sort out the issues in my life," "to come to terms with the world's issues," "to try to answer the big questions," "to add my opinion to the debate," "to organize my thoughts so that I understand them myself," and "to figure out what I really think." He read quickly, ignoring the names on the title page, circling only the most irritating errors and writing only a brief comment at the end of each essay. He found one essay so inspiring that he read to the last paragraph without marking the paper:

> When I started college, I thought writing was nothing more than a simple exercise, like walking along a well-lit, well-marked path in a safe and shady park in a small city. Someone else designed the path, and all I had to do was stay off the grass. Now I feel like I'm standing at the middle of a suspension bridge, my toes curled over the edge, a bungee cord tied around my ankles, the river flowing fast and furiously two-hundred feet below me. I could wait here forever, but to write is to jump, to take the chance, to do something besides stand and watch the river run by. Okay. Here goes.

Without looking, Watkins knew who wrote it. Humbled by the power of the writing, grateful that he wouldn't have to find the words to express his reactions, he scratched an A+ on the last page. Just then the phone rang.

*God damn,* he thought and picked up the receiver. "Hello."

"Peter."

He was certain of the voice. "Diane."

There was a momentary silence, and Watkins felt he should fill the void. "Uh, Diane, I, uh, how are you?"

"Peter, your letter is beautiful. Why didn't you ever tell me?"

"I thought you knew."

"Who could tell with you? Sometimes I thought *maybe*, but you, I thought you considered me a sister. You were always so thoughtful, but I, I just never knew."

"I'm sorry, I shouldn't have said those things in the letter. I shouldn't have, I uh, I'm sorry."

"Why? Didn't you mean them?"

"No, I mean yes, I mean, yes, I meant them. I'm just saying I'm sorry to put you on the spot. I uh ..."

"Don't be sorry. I wouldn't have called if I were offended. I'm glad you took the risk. I think we should get together and, you know, talk and whatever."

"What about Ridge?"

"Ridge who?"

"Ridge who?! Ridge! Ridge from the postcard! I was guessing it was Ridge Rowlands."

"What are you talking about, Peter?"

Watkins thought he was being toyed with. He walked over to his desk and searched through the rubble. "I have it right here. You sent me a postcard that says, "Pete—Got your letter. You're right— been in the library every day with RIDGE. I was glad to hear from you, etc. etc."

"I don't even know Ridge Rowlands. Isn't he that rich kid studying Hemingway? Like I would go out with someone studying Hemingway! I can't believe. . . ." She stopped. "Peter."

"Yeah."

"You psychotic! The card says COLERIDGE! I've been in the library everyday with Coleridge! Remember him? The subject of my dissertation? I must have hyphenated his name on the card and you read too fast."

Watkins looked at the postcard. Sure enough, Diane had split the name into its syllables, and the first had been obliterated by the postmark. Had he been a little less anxious, he would have noticed it. Having not noticed it on the first reading, he was bound to miss it every time thereafter. He wasn't sure of what to say.

"Oh."

Diane was laughing. "'Oh'? Peter. 'Oh'? You drive yourself into a state of hysteria and that's your response? 'Oh'? Pretty lame for an English teacher."

"I mean, Oh, yeah."

Together they laughed and talked for hours. Diane's news toward the end of the conversation thrilled Watkins. "I have a good shot at a school only a few miles from where you're teaching, Peter. Eighty-two miles, in fact."

"An hour's drive for you."

"I've slowed down. If I get the position you can visit me and show me how to teach writing."

"Oh, no," Watkins returned. "If I discover *that* secret, I'm writing the book and retiring."

"Publishers have deadlines."

"Okay, the outline."

# Wednesday, December 10

## John

"Thanks for waiting with me, Nick. She should be here any minute."

"Don't be crazy. I won't be seeing you for a while. It's good to spend a few last minutes with you. Do you have big plans for the holidays? We always go to our aunt's on Christmas day. She puts out this huge spread. Takes so long to eat we don't get home till the new year. It's good food, though. Besides, she loves it when we're there. The house is filled with people. And with my sister's baby, this'll be a great Christmas. It's always more fun when kids are around. Hey, did I tell you Jen and I rented a few old movies the other night, a couple of those Bogart films you recommended? Good choice. Jen loved them."

"I'm glad Jen's parents were so good about you."

"I must admit I was surprised. Her father is a bit shocked. I think he'll be harder to win over, but her mother was great. Says as long as I'm good to Jen and she loves me, it doesn't matter to her in the least."

"People can really surprise you," John said. "Her father'll come along when he realizes you're his daughter's best chance to escape that last name."

"I'm taking her name," Nick said, "so I can name our first son Oscar Meyer."

John's laughter trailed off into a giggle as his mother pulled her Tercel to the curb where he and Nick sat. "Hi, Mom," he called out as she got out of the car. He went over and kissed her. "We're going to run up for the rest of my stuff." As they walked to the room, Nick and John talked about the semester. "I got real lucky meeting you, Nick," John said, trying to fight the tears. "I don't think I would have made it through this semester without you. You're a great friend. I think you're going to be a wonderful teacher."

"What are you trying to do, Johnny Mariner, make me cry?"

When they got to the room, Nick went in first, flinging open the door so that it headed directly for the desk chair but catching it just in time. "Good teacher, slow learner," he said smiling. "Is this all you have left?" Nick asked picking up a duffel bag stuffed with laundry.

"Yep, that's it. I can take it, Nick. You better go over and see if Jen needs help. Come back to the car in a few minutes, though and say goodbye."

When John reached the car he tossed the laundry bundle on the backseat.

"Oh, for me, John? You shouldn't have!" his mother said.

"Now, Mom, did you really think I'd come home empty handed?"

John's mother opened her door and settled into the driver's seat. "Well," she said to John through the open passenger's door, "should we get going?"

John sat down. "Do you mind waiting a few minutes, Mom? Nick said he'd come back to say goodbye. It should only be a moment."

His mother said she didn't mind waiting. "Beside, I never got to meet him. Remember, he never made it to Parents' Weekend."

"Oh, that's right," John replied. He spotted Nick running toward the car. "Well, here he comes. You can meet him now. Here he comes."

"Where?"

"Right there."

"Where?"

John stepped out of the car, and his mother followed. Nick slowed and came to a stop directly in front of John. "I'm glad you waited. I thought I'd have to chase the car."

"You'd probably catch it, too," John said. He extended his hand, "Well, I'll see you in a few weeks, Roomie."

Nick looked down at John's hand, then at John's face. Suddenly he threw his massive arms around John, one over his left shoulder and the other around his right side, hugged him and slapped him several times on the back. John's feet were a few inches off the ground. "I'm going to miss you, Johnny Mariner. You be good." He let go.

Released, John stumbled backward, only half-kidding that he couldn't catch his breath. Nick laughed.

"Nick, I want you to meet my mother."

By this point, Joy was standing alongside the car staring in dis-believe at the sight before her. Nick stepped toward her with his arms out as if he were about to repeat the crushing affection he had just shown John. When he got close enough, he grabbed her hand. "I'm happy to meet you, John's mother."

"I'm happy to meet you, too, John's roommate," she responded. She just stood there, her mouth open.

"Mom. MOM!"

"What?"

"Let's go." She settled slowly into the car.

"See you, Nick," John said. I didn't think it'd be this hard to say goodbye."

"If that car leaves and you're not in it, you'll regret it," Nick said, "maybe not today, maybe not tomorrow, but soon, and for the rest of your life."

John laughed. "That's a lousy impersonation."

"Goodbye, John."

"Goodbye, Nick."

As they pulled away from the curb, John's mother looked over at him, at the road in front of her, and back at John. "Why didn't you ever tell me?" she asked.

"Tell you what, Ma?"

"Tell me that your roommate was black?"

"Huh? Oh, I guess it just never came up. By-the-way, Mom?"

Joy still appeared stunned. "Yes."

"Will you teach me to dance?"

# LEARNING GUIDE

Questions and Topics for
Writing, Thinking and Understanding the Novel

# Learning Guide

This guide contains questions, topics and ideas for using the novel in critical thinking and writing classes. The guide begins with a brief introduction for each of the five categories of questions covered in the guide: *Questions for Critical Thinking, The Writing Process, Topics for Writing, Questions for Discussion, and Understanding the Novel.* Following this introduction is a chapter-by-chapter list of questions and topics. Critical thinking instructors may find useful questions in the other four sections, and *vice versa.* Occasionally, if it is applicable to both critical thinking and writing, a question is repeated in two sections. Finally, many of the questions under Chapter 5 are relevant to the entire novel. (All numbers in parentheses refer to pages in the novel.)

### Questions for Critical Thinking

In reading a novel set on a college campus, students are invited to practice their critical thinking skills by examining and evaluating the behavior and reasoning of fictional characters, some of whom may reflect the reader's own tendency to generalize, stereotype, draw hasty conclusions, make unwarranted assumptions, judge without evidence, evaluate without criteria, appeal unfairly to emotions, and so forth. In the questions that appear in this learning guide under the heading Questions for Critical Thinking, students are asked to examine not only the logic but also the habits of mind of the characters and to provide examples when their own logic or habits have paralleled those they encounter in John, Eileen, Professor Watkins, Dr. Sally Sprego, and others. Readers of the novel should be alert to evidence of prejudice, bias, and presumptiveness in both the characters and themselves. The novel contains a number of examples of fallacious reasoning and weak arguments that vigilant readers will quickly identify.

The first chapter of the novel presents an opportunity for young thinkers to examine the question of their identity—to determine what influences and conditions have contributed to their unique way of seeing the world. The subsequent chapters contain conversations among and between various characters, conversations that contain examples of both faulty and clear reasoning. Among the key critical thinking ideas and themes in the novel are that the journey toward becoming a critical thinker begins with self-discovery, that knowledge without action is fruitless, that assumptions built on the scantiest evidence can debilitate a thinker, that critical reasoning is not diametrically opposed to emotion, and that the ability to evaluate fairly is the most difficult faculty for a critical thinker to achieve.

### The Writing Process

Eileen's recognition of herself as a "teenage daughter of a dead mother" illustrates the central concept of the writing process espoused in this book. While much of writing is, of necessity, formal and objective, the attainment of good writing must start with looking within—examining how we think and feel about that which directly affects us. John's writing will initially offer a contrast to Eileen's in that it relies on imagination to "escape" his reality: interesting and technically more competent, it deprives the writer the ability as in Eileen's case to take the first step toward coming to terms with a serious problem. For Eileen writing becomes therapeutic; John's evasive approach, however, prevents him from truly getting in touch with his feelings, an essential initial step which might have led him earlier to the discovery that writing can both identify problems and encourage the action necessary to overcome or deal with than appropriately.

While writing teachers often despair of the possibility of eradicating comma splices, notice that the initial question, "Who am I?"—one infrequently asked in any other course—sparks a response that saves a student from quitting at the very outset of her college career. Once students internalize the value of writing, they can more easily be encouraged to "clean-up" the exteriors—even comma splices

In terms of exploring the topic, Who am I," Watkins is clearly correct in asserting that everyone "has something to say." Each person is an expert on this topic and can attain solid ground. Determining what is most interesting, sincere, and important, however, can be achieved by brainstorming, developing a thesis, and outlining (for without structure even an inspirational "jewel of an idea" can be lost). The process is two-fold: 1) students need to discover what is worth exploring and saying; and 2) they need to learn how to say it most effectively. Some students will complain that outlining and other initial steps are "boring," but if they do not buy into the pre-writing process, they will not ultimately achieve a good writing *product*.

The initial assignment attempts to assess what ideas the students have and how they develop them. They are urged to write freely without fear of a grade. It works immediately for Eileen who poignantly explores and analyzes her situation, concluding "I want to have a mother." Jennifer, on the other hand, misses the real point of what she wants to say—not the love of a career in travel but the understandable desire "to get out." For this exercise Watkins will identify the "jewel of an idea" or at least lead the way; later working in groups, the students will be encouraged to articulate in a clearer fashion, invaluable in the pre-writing process. In the early stage of group work, the goal is for students to become more comfortable with each other; later, they should trust each other to offer the objective criticism which is so helpful in the process of moving from draft to draft.

### Topics for Writing

This learning guide contains numerous writing topics drawn from the specific events and ideas presented in the novel. These topics primarily focus on a student's experiences as they reflect or differ from those of the characters.

### Questions for Discussion

While many of the questions in this category continue the focus of those in Topics for Writing, many others are more global or general and ask students to respond to the ethical and social issues addressed in the novel. Some of the questions in this section could be used as paper topics for essays assigned later in the course.

### Understanding the Novel

These questions invite readers to examine the novel's plot, characters and themes, and to give their personal reactions to the text as literature.

# CHAPTER I

*Questions for Critical Thinking*

1. The first chapter of *Parallel Lives* focuses on the identity of the characters, or more accurately how the characters attempt to identify themselves. Since John participated in nothing beyond the classroom, in some ways he has no existence. No one knows him. How do you identify yourself? What face do you show the world? How do you *like* to be perceived?

2. Our identities are often formed by experience and influence. What influences have contributed to make you who you are? Where are you from? What was your home life like? What is your economic class, your religion, your work experience, and so forth? Do you think these influences distinguish you from your classmates? What traits do you feel you share with your classmates and other members of your generation? What have you experienced that is unique or unusual?

3. How do you think you are perceived by others, by your friends, your parents, your teachers, strangers? What contributes to the assessment of you that others make? Think about some concrete examples of times in which you have been completely misunderstood or misjudged. Have you ever felt that the impression you've given is exactly the opposite of how you really are. For example, has your shyness ever been mistaken for arrogance or aloofness? Has there ever been a time when you have consciously attempted to alter your identity, to pretend to be someone you are not? What was the result?

4. Consider what each person on the left side of the following list concludes about the person on the right side. What evidence does each use to come to his or her conclusion:

    JOHN about WATKINS
    WATKINS about JOHN
    JOHN about Eileen
    EILEEN about WATKINS
    WATKINS about Eileen
    WATKINS about THE STUDENTS IN HIS CLASS

5. What do you, as the reader, know about these characters that the other characters do not know? What evidence do you have for making judgments?

6. Eileen listens to a radio show on her commute home. Whenever you encounter this show in the novel, examine the reasoning of the psychologist and her callers. In the example given on page 15, Sally demonstrates several errors in logic when she asks the caller "What was your fantasy?" Do you think that Sally shows a lack of empathy for the caller? Should Sally empathize in this case?

7. After Eileen's conversation with Tony and Gary, she listens again to the radio show (27-28). Evaluate the conversation between Sally and the caller over whether two members of different religions can have a happy marriage. Can you find errors in both Sally's and the caller's reasoning?

8. What appeals are made in the MateFind advertisement (28)?

9. Arriving home, Eileen watches a few minutes of a talk show (29). Evaluate Mrs. Gorshinski's views on the death penalty. Eileen understands the emotions behind the argument, but is it logical?

10. You might try listening to radio call-in shows, watching talk shows, examining advertisements for more examples of faulty reasoning. Why, do you think, these media sources are such gold mines of illogic and covert emotional appeals?

11. John's tends to invent an identity (as he does when trying to get out of playing tennis) because he worries about what others will think of him. In fact, he has sometimes lied to avoid participating in the events of his life. He'd rather come up with an excuse than get involved. Can you recall ever having done the same thing? Why is it that many of us would rather fabricate a story than experience something we may find uncomfortable or difficult?

12. Watkins and John tend to see things in black and white terms; they sometimes categorize people into two groups. Give some examples of this tendency and show what other possibilities exist.

13. At the end of the chapter, John approaches Watkins to ask about a grade. Is this a realistic portrayal of a college student? Why are grades so important? As the novel progresses, watch for the theme of evaluation and grading.

14. After you've read the chapter, ask yourself how well you know who you are. All of us filter the world through our personal lenses. What are yours? Does knowing *who* we are help us understand *how* we see the world?

### The Writing Process

1. Having read Eileen's essay (25-26), Watkins cannot find the "words to express how moving and honest the writing was, how touching without being maudlin." Do you agree with this description? What are some of the elements that are moving and honest?

2. If you were a member of Eileen's group, would you have a similar reaction to that of Tony and Gary? What does this say about the potential of writing to reveal ourselves to others? What does it suggest about the power of words?

3. Does Eileen's paper meet the requirements of "saying what you want to say" (14)? Compare her paper to Jennifer's initial exercise (24-25). Does Watkins correctly identify the "jewel of an idea"? In what ways does John's paper (41-42) fall short of these goals?

4. While John is capable of writing a "well-organized and flawlessly structured paper" (17), technically Eileen's paper is not as effective in terms of a clear topic sentence, neat transitions, and, to be sure, grammatical accuracy. If you were able to touch the reader as effectively as Eileen does, however, would this give you more incentive to learn the technical parts that would help to make you a truly effective writer?

5. Students must try to "free themselves from the fear of being evaluated and censured," Watkins proclaims (21). Does this fear

often prevent you from thinking freely enough about you topic? Does it inhibit your ability to express yourself?

6. In the same passage cited in question 5, Watkins implores his students "to find their voices." Has Eileen found her voice? By definition does finding one's voice mean looking honestly within yourself—discovering your true feelings and getting in touch with who you are?

7. Do you agree with the emphasis Watkins places on the "jewel of an idea?" Can you see that developing this "jewel" frees you to "say what you want to say" and to express yourself more freshly and originally?

8. Some students see groups, outlining, and brainstorming as "cluttering up" the writing process. If Jennifer, however, were to take these elements seriously, could she end up saying what she wants to say more effectively in her final paper (24-25)? Would she, indeed, arrive at a better understanding of "who she is"?

9. What does the essay, "Who am I?" do for Eileen? Would you agree that writing, because if forces us to come to terms with our feelings and thoughts, can at the best of times be therapeutic? If your own writing could have an effect on you similar to Eileen's, would this be another incentive for you to work at writing more effectively?

10. Surprisingly, Watkins describes his own writing as "lousy" as he compares it to a piece of writing of the novelist, Barbara Kingsolver (24). He is probably expressing the idea that we can never be quite the good writers we would like to be. How far, though, do you think the ideas presented by Watkins can take us? Consider being "honest," finding one's voice, saying what you want to say, brainstorming, and capturing the "jewel of an idea."


*Topics for Writing*

1. As a starting point for your writing this semester, try your hand at the exercise Professor Watkins assigns on the first day of class. Just follow the directions on page 14.

2. Another approach to identifying who you are and perhaps to introducing yourself to your group, is to write an essay in which you discuss one or two things you like about yourself and one or two things you do not like. Do a combination of three in all, devoting equal attention to each item. Try to illustrate the characteristics fully; for instance, if you have a problem with procrastination, show how it has sometimes made things unpleasant or uncomfortable.

3. Jumping quickly to the wrong conclusion, John initially imagines Eileen to be a "rich, arrogant girl" (13). Clearly, the author shows us how far John is off the mark. Consider an experience in which you, too, initially judged a situation or person incorrectly. What may have led you to the first assessment? Compare how different this first impression was from your later realizations.

4. Just as we sometimes don't see other people correctly, other people, in turn, may make wrong assumptions about us. If you are shy, for instance, others might think you are unfriendly or snobbish. Try to illustrate instances in which others got a wrong impression about you; or perhaps you might want to tackle a combination—as suggested in question 2—of how they are right in one or two areas and wrong in one or two.

5. Paralleling the anxiety Eileen and John experience as new students, Professor Watkins feels "knots the size of baseballs" as he faces his first year as an assistant professor. Write an essay illustrating how you react to a new situation either as challenging or threatening. Perhaps you would like to contrast both a challenging and a threatening experience

6. When they are attracted to "a gorgeous woman," most guys, John theorizes, fall into two categories (13) You may or not subscribe to the notion that there are, indeed, two such "camps." Do you, for instance, find this generalization to be too simplistic? Do you believe men and women can approach each other with more naturalness, less role playing, and more honesty?

7. Recalling an embarrassing moment when he got caught "checking out a girl" (13), John still vividly remembers that he "turned away so quickly . . . that he cracked his head." Some embarrassing moments appear funny afterwards but at the time may be

painful, unpleasant, and even mortifying. Describe an embarrassing moment you have had, trying to explain the situation clearly and dealing fully with the emotions you experienced.

8. Following the humorous but baffling tennis incident, Nick insists that honesty is essential to a special relationship. Would you agree that this, along with other factors, is essential for two people to become best friends? Write a paper in which you explore three categories: buddies (you may play sports with or participate in some activity); acquaintances (they may be neighbors but not real close); and friends (with whom you have a strong bond).

9. John makes certain assumptions about Nick's choices of posters lining the walls of their dorm room. Your parents, for instance, may make assumptions (and perhaps be puzzled by) your choices of music, clothes, books, films, etc. Write a paper explaining what your choices in one or more of these areas reveal about you.

10. Consider John's statement beginning "All weekend he'd taken note of the various means by which his companions established their identity" (39). You may find this a fair assessment or exaggerated, but write your own essay in which you explore how you choose to establish your own identity.

### Questions for Discussion

1. Sitting in a college classroom for the first time, John has the feeling that this experience is "like an alarm clock going off on the morning of his adult life" (page 4). At the end of the chapter, Watkins exclaims: "There's more to college than just grades." (42) At this early phase in your college career,' how do you respond to these quotes? Do you see college as a new phase or as a continuation of high school?

2. John's fear of speaking in class is so intense that he wanted his mother to lie for him at his high school graduation(5) . Discuss anxieties you may have about speaking or other types of anxieties you may have in a group situation. Do you make an attempt

to overcome these fears? If you do, explain what steps you take. If you do not, what are the consequences?

3.  Looking back at how you responded to question 1, now that you are at college, do you agree with John that there are "dangers of appearing too eager, too interested or too entertained" (6)? Is this response to peer pressure an attitude that can be left behind in high school?

4.  Are you surprised that Professor Watkins, a proven scholar and teacher, "had knots in his stomach the size of baseballs" (7)? Consider the following questions: 1) do we create stereotypes about teachers that prevent us from seeing that they might be nervous and vulnerable (after all, they know so much and wield grading power); and 2) do we assume that some people must "have it made" (they're smarter, richer, more competent), and so they must be sure of themselves and perfectly confident?

5.  With the Phillies losing by fifteen runs, Watkins "finished his coffee, watered his plants, shaved, called his sister, and cleaned the bathroom. With nothing to distract or entice him, he returned to Jennifer's essay" (22-23). Many people are "afflicted" with procrastination. How would you describe your own work habits? Consider habits that are good, bad, and could use improvement. Do this question right now.

6.  Compare/contrast John's attitude towards groups ("In his mind, John glared at Watkins and wished him dead" (22) with Eileen's (GROUPS! The word struck Eileen like a gentle breeze" (26)). What do their respective attitudes towards group situations reveal about the personalities of these two characters?

7.  Remembering her mother's warning "that her good looks might intimidate men," Eileen thinks about Tony Falcone and wonders "Maybe I should do the asking" (29). Do you believe it would be "proper" for Eileen to break the unwritten rule that men should do the asking? How observant should we be to the roles assigned men and women?

8.  After showing himself to be "a geek with no athleticism" (33) John expects "brutal razzing full of vulgarity" from Nick but is rather "baffled" by Nick's "maturity." "'Why did you lie to me?' Nick asked provoked but clearly more concerned that he had been de-

ceived by someone he had trusted." Consider the following questions: does our need to be well thought of inhibit us from being honest with one another? and 2) does a real friendship demand such honesty?

9. Eileen sees the need to encourage her sister, Maury, even at the young age of ten, "to make a move without someone's approval"...and "to think for herself and take risks" (37) Looking back at question one again, are these some of the qualities essential to adulthood?

10. Again referring to question 1, is it possible that Watkins's final comment in the chapter that "there is more to college than just grades" (42) is more than a truism that is easy for teachers to pronounce? Does the need to succeed in college and in career opportunities down the line dictate the absolute all-importance of grades? Or is Watkins correct in his philosophy that learning is not only about someone's evaluation of our work?

### Understanding the Novel

1. At the outset of the novel, both John and Professor Watkins experience something entirely new—John, his first day of college, and Watkins, his first official day as an assistant professor. They share parallels in other particulars as well: shyness, insecurity, and self-consciousness. Cite examples to substantiate this statement.

2. At this stage in the novel, do you think it would be accurate to describe both Watkins and John as loners, as outsiders? What indications do you find?

3. In contrast to John's hyper-shyness and insecurity, as Nick bolts through the door like a whirlwind (p.11), he exhibits a personality absolutely opposite: sure of himself, outgoing, and in-charge. Which character, if either, most accurately reflects the personality of a first-year student?

4. Looking at the first paragraph of page 20, discuss some insights that this passage may provide about what challenges a sensitive teacher may face?

5. In John's writing group, Jeremy remarks: "I really like the one about having nothing to do. I agree. This town sucks" (23). How does this feeling of the students parallel Watkins's reaction to the town? Do you think the author might be suggesting something about the relationship of satisfaction or happiness to geography?

6. What does the writer reveal about Watkins in the scene (25-26) in which he reads Eileen's paper? Why does he call his mother? Note parallels of John and his mother (4) and his calling home "after a bout of homesickness" (39). What might the author be suggesting at this point?

7. Compare the reaction Watkins has to Eileen's paper with the re-action of the students in the group. Why does the author seem to draw this parallel?

8. What parallels do you see being made between matters dis-cussed in questions 6 and 7 with the conversation between Eileen and Maury on page 38?

9. What "gem" does Watkins discover in John's paper (41-42), and what do you think may be suggested by John's insistence: "Well, that's not going to happen." Why does John appear to be so adamant about this point?

10. After his drinking binge (39). John reflects that he could become "the Cinderella college kid trading the anonymity or disdain that scholarship brings for the notoriety and respect that come with drunkenness and haziness." John's desire to be more "accept-able" to the group is understandable, but is this a reasonable ap-proach?

11. Expressing more desire than confidence, initially John remarks to his mother: "This phase might help me, you know, get along bet-ter—a baptism of fire" (4). What progress do you see John mak-ing in the course of this first chapter?

12. Watkins mistakenly believes that "using his charm and power of persuasion," he has convinced Eileen "to stay for a week and try

the first assignment." But actually Eileen at first has "no intention of doing anything of the sort" (11). Cite other examples in the chapter in which characters make wrong assumptions about the actions or intentions of other characters.

13. At first glance, John and Eileen may not appear very much alike. But what parallels do you see in their personalities or situation? Does this have some bearing on why Eileen finally decides to stay in college?

# CHAPTER II

*Questions for Critical Thinking*

1. John's preoccupation with grades continues at the start of Chapter 2 (45). He hasn't been given the grades he feels he deserves, and he begins to search for explanations. Look at some of his reasoning. Why is his thinking so fuzzy at this point? Look carefully at his arguments: Watkins doesn't favor girls, John believes, because Jen is getting C's. He should be doing better since he likes to write. Watkins must have changed his mind about John's abilities. What is wrong with John's reasoning in arriving at each of these conclusions?

2. In their conversation (47-48), Eileen's grandmother tells her why women often weren't educated in the past. What reason does she give? What fallacy is this an example of? Is the grandmother guilty of fallacious reasoning?

3. Evaluate some of the language used by the talk show host and Dr. Sally (49-51). Do such terms as "liberal mainstream media" or "misguided critics" do anything to advance our understanding of the issues at hand? Is the use of these terms illogical or fallacious?

4. When asked why people might disagree with her, Sally claims that they don't like to hear the truth or that they can't face life honestly (49). What's wrong with her defense?

5. Although she claims to have learned from her mistakes, neither Sally nor the host seems to see a problem with preaching one thing and doing another. Is it always hypocritical to act in a manner different from the way we expect others to act? Is hypocrisy illogical?

6. Examine the statement "No one seems to realize that they alone are responsible for who they are, what they do, what happens to them and what they become" (50). Do you agree with this statement? How does this statement compare to the points made by Eileen's grandmother a few pages earlier?

7.  Sally illustrates the point that children should be disciplined by referring to a caller who found a thirteen-year-old sleeping in her home (50). Is Sally ignoring anything in her advice to the caller? Has she considered the "complexities" and possibilities of the issue? Sally uses her own experiences to defend her conclusions? Is this fair?

8.  Sally believes that problems would be fewer with parents at home (50-51). Is she right? How about the problems she lists? Is it logical to argue that these problems will lessen if families remain intact?

9.  In grading Gary Kardell's essay, Watkins records a C- even though he admits to himself that it "deserves" no more than a D+. Do you think Watkins is making a mistake in grading according to his assumptions about Gary's feelings and reactions? Sally believes that we worry too much about "self esteem" and that people must be responsible for their actions? What would Sally most likely say about Watkins's grading methods at this point? What would you do in Watkins's position? Do you fell that he has violated his standards for evaluating an essay?

10. When Nick reads about the racial incident, he becomes angry (70). On what basis does he establish Tony Falcone's guilt? Is he being fair?

11. Carefully examine the discussion that takes place in the classroom concerning the racial incident. Comment on the following points raised by students.

    - Is it racist to call a white man by his first name and a black man by his last? (71)

    - Do you agree, with some Native Americans, that sports teams should not be named after groups of people who might find those names offensive? (71)

    - Are all members of a class or race or group responsible for the behavior or some members? Is the behavior of some members a reflection on the larger group? (72)

- Is Peter Churnip right to suggest that noticing the accomplishments of African Americans is a subtle form of racism? (72)

- Is the newspaper usually a trustworthy source of information or of people's comments? Are newspapers objective? (74)

- Is Eileen correct in suggesting that the interview of witnesses may have been flawed? (74)

- Is Watkins correct in claiming that the meaning of some words depends on their context (74)? Consider a word like "doll." How might the meaning of that word depend on context—who says it, when, where, to whom? Can you think of any other words that have different meanings in different contexts?

12. The conclusion of the discussion between Watkins and his students seems to be that lacking sensitivity is racist. In other words, if we do nothing *deliberately* offensive, we can still be charged with having a racist nature if we act with indifference toward others. Do you believe that this is true? If we offend someone not of our race and defend ourselves by saying "I just wasn't thinking," can we be charged with racism? Is racism always a *conscious* bias toward other races? Is Peter Churnip correct in suggesting that we can be racist without *knowing* it?

13. John is preoccupied with Eileen's relationship to Tony and her availability. He has trouble concentrating on the issue. He is surprised that Chris's comments anger Watkins even though Watkins has no personal involvement. Jen seems especially angry at people who don't care about events that don't involve them directly. Whose attitude to you most associate with? Do you agree that we tend to be more interested in issues that directly affect us? Do you feel that you should concern yourself only with issues that personally involve you?

14. Robert Henderson's comment that some people "expect to be treated with racism" is one that is often heard. Do you agree with him?

15. Can you provide a clear, logical, unbiased definition of feminism, sexism, chauvinism and racism?

16. The conversation between Watkins and Tony is not revealed until after the class discussion on racism. During the class, Watkins had information he withheld. (In fact, because of the structure of the novel, the information was withheld from the reader as well.) Should Watkins have done this? Can a teacher be "dishonest" to prove a point? Does knowing what Tony said to Watkins alter your conclusion about whether or not he acted in a racist manner?

### *The Writing Process*

1. Reading the first line of Gary Kardell's essay provokes Watkins into fantasizing about driving a tractor trailer "all over the country terrorizing people in small cares" (53). Compose a thesis sentence for Gary's essay that is more effective stylistically and identifies more concretely three things about "my generation."

2. If John were to accept Watkins's advice "to put yourself into your writing," what self- discovery might be possible in relation to Watkins's comment: "I get the feeling, John, that what you're really talking about is the kind of intolerance, prejudice, and cruelty that you've experienced because you feel that you're different from everyone else" (62-63)?

3. Assessing some shortcomings in John's paper, Watkins advises: "Don't write that everyone your age is intolerant; write that you have been treated with intolerance" (63). If John took this advice, in what ways would he end up with a better paper?

4. What is it in John's writing that leads Watkins to assert the need for him to find his own voice? In what respect does it appear that John has resisted this advice?

5. Even though they were written for different assignments, you can compare John's paper with Eileen's (80-81). In what ways does she follow Watkins's advice to John in finding her voice, taking risks, and being honest?

6. Explaining to Watkins a problem writing the third paper, Eileen states that "writing about my family was too difficult; there's too much sadness. . . . I just couldn't" (66-67). Together they decide that she should "complete the assignment with an illustrative essay on her little sister's personality." Consider the following questions: 1) why was it good advice to try a different slant; and 2) how does the final paper so encompass good writing process that Watkins can exclaim about teaching: "It just got better"? (80)

## *Topics for Writing*

1. Although "Hootie had fallen out of fashion," [Eileen] still enjoyed the music, and some of the songs spoke to her personally." (Some readers familiar with the album may know why.) Write a paper in which you discuss how your favorite music speaks to you as it does to the character, Eileen. Be sure to give the reader a clear sense of what the music "says" and "how it sounds" as well as how you respond to it.

2. Eileen "sometimes got the impression that her grandmother didn't truly understand what college work entailed" (47-48). Compare and contrast in several areas what you have found to be the reality of college with what your parents may believe.

3. Discussing the role of women in her grandmother's day, Eileen realizes that she has opportunities that were not afforded previous generations. Compare and contrast the opportunities you have with that of your parents and/or grandparents.

4. The term, "feminism," is bandied about by various characters in this chapter. Write a paper in which you define what you think the term means.

5. "The hardest thing for a young person to do," claims John, "is to take a stand against the group or to disagree with what everyone else is saying" (55). Discuss a situation in which you dared to stand up against a person or group. Explain the situation fully; what were you feelings at each stage of the encounter?

6. "We should be able to forgive one another for isolated cases of insensitivity," Eileen asserts in the class discussion on racism (76). Write a paper in which you describe a situation when you were insensitive, or one in which someone was insensitive to you. Do you agree that we can forgive "isolated cases of insensitivity"?

7. Much of the chapter has been concerned with the description of Watkins as teacher. Write a category paper in which you illustrate three distinct types of teachers with whom you have come into contact. Or you might wish to consider three types of students or athletes.

### Questions for Discussion

1. Complementing the discussion of racism in this chapter is a short discussion between Eileen and her grandmother (47-49) and an interview with the radio psychologist (50-51) on the role of women. What is Eileen's position on feminism as opposed to those of her grandmother and the radio psychologist? What is your position?

2. Agonizing over a grade for Gary's paper, Watkins reflects that "grading someone's writing was the hardest of all" (57). Do you agree? In general do you concur with the discourse on grading presented in this passage?

3. Looking at the passage on page 61 that begins: "Every graduate school should offer a course in how to teach," do you believe that questioning one's ability and performance is natural and perhaps necessary if a person wants to do a good job?

4. Do the areas covered in questions two and three give you reason to re-assess possible stereotype notions you may have about teachers?

5. Though he falls short of "how English professors are always portrayed—giving inspiring lectures . . . reaching a powerful crescendo just as the period ends, arousing the women, humbling the men" (61), how do you assess Watkins's talent. In his discussion with John (62-64), does he, from the student's point of view, "get it right"? Simply stated, as a student would you want this teacher?

6. "It occurs to me that we could define racism to include a lack of empathy," Watkins states (76). What instances of lack of empathy do you see in society or in your own community? Is this lack of empathy a matter of concern to you?

### Understanding the Novel

1. While John's hesitancy to speak to Watkins about his grades hurts only himself, his unwillingness or inability to speak up hurts Jennifer and irritates Nick (71). John fails to support Jennifer even though she appears to take a position on the racial incident reflected in John's paper: "When young people lose the ability to imagine what it's like to be someone else, they have an easier time hurting others." In other words, Jen seems to be the very kind of person John admires: she can imagine the pain of someone else. And yet, he himself does nothing to support her during the class discussion. How do you account for this inconsistency?

2. About the same time John is blaming Watkins for his "low" grade (45-46), Eileen hears the radio psychologist proclaim: "I'm trying to get people to take responsibility for their own lives, to stop them from blaming everything and everybody else. . ." (50). Do you see a meaningful connection?

3. As evidenced by the first paragraph of page 52, what are some of the sources of Watkins's anxiety?

4.   Theorizing that students "probably thought that professors enjoyed grading. . ." and that it offered "the opportunity to fail a paper, to drive a stake through the heart of some miserable student" (53-54), Watkins reflects on his actual view of grading. What does this view of grading reveal about him?

5.   At this point in the novel, would it appear wise for John to take Watkins's advice: "Why not write about how it feels to be an outsider, to live outside the group, whether the group has banished you or you've exiled yourself?" (63)

6.   Defying his own advice to his students "to say what you want to say," Watkins sends his letter to Diane "despite knowing that it said nothing that he wanted to say." Does he contradict his own theory that writing can get you involved, can be a means of action, and can encourage you to take risks?

7.   We see different points of view expressed in this chapter and the next on racism. How would you characterize Jennifer's point of view? Is it more passionately expressed than other points that are presented by the various students?

8.   Having told Diane: "I love this job," and then later : "It just got better," Watkins hears Gary ask: "I was just wondering if we did anything important today." Why does the author juxtapose these comments?

9.   Not afraid to criticize but also always there for support, advice, and encouragement, Nick is a "model" friend to John. Do you agree? What does the author suggest about the value of friendship.

# CHAPTER III

## *Questions for Critical Thinking*

1.  The students in Watkins's class begin to give him a hard time over his methods, though one gets the feeling that Theodore is simply having fun or that he's trying to turn the tables on Watkins. Do you think his mock abuse of the class is as bad or as offensive as some of the students suggest? Whether you think Watkins's methods are uncalled for, the point that a professor has power in the class in an interesting one. Do you think that Theodore and the others are out of line in their challenge to Watkins's authority? How far would you go in challenging authority? Should Watkins assert his authority; should he come on stronger at this point?

2.  Some students equate Watkins's outburst with such methods as the one Belinda mentions—where a supposed robber bursts into the room—and Stanley Milgram's famous experiment. The comparisons may or may not be fair, but clearly some students feel that proving a point or teaching a lesson or discovering information has its limits. How far would you go to make a point? If you felt strongly that you were right about something, how far would you go to convince someone of your point of view?

3.  Watkins's methods raise another issue. Because he apparently believes that it is difficult for us to empathize with people of different races, he is trying to create in his students the same feeling that Jim Washington might have experienced. Do you agree that experience is the best teacher? Is it possible for us to know the feelings and reactions of people whose lives are different from our own? Can a doctor know how intense his or her patient's pain is if the doctor has never experienced it? Can we know what it means to be homeless or hungry if we're born into a wealthy family? Is it possible for someone to simply imagine what another person feels? Can empathy come from imagination?

4.  If you believe that the deepest empathy results from experience, do you think that you can teach someone to empathize? How far would you go to create an empathy-teaching experience for an-

other person?  For example, suppose that another driver were tailgating you.  Would you let that driver pass and then ride his or her bumper to show them what it feels like to drive with someone on your tail?  Do you think it would work?  Would you hit a child to let the child know that hitting causes other people pain?  Would you steal to punish a thief?  Have you seen the commercial for United Air Lines in which customer service representatives are left waiting for their boss?  He arrives late to show them how uncomfortable waiting is.  Do you think people who are given "a taste of their own medicine" learn a lesson?

5.  The question Watkins leaves his students with is an important one that never gets answered in the novel.  Judging on the information provided to the students through the newspaper account—in other words, without knowing Tony's intentions or Jim's feelings—do you feel that Tony's actions constitute "hate speech" as defined by the college code?  How would you judge the case if you were on a disciplinary board?  Does your own school have regulations governing speech and behavior?

6.  Belinda raises an interesting point about censorship.  She finds certain T-shirts offensive and suggests that they be banned?  Is she right?  College students and other young people seem to get away with wearing slogans and logos on their clothing that might be considered offensive in some circles.  Would you argue for censoring certain items of clothing?  Why or why not?

7.  This third chapter contains a lengthy section on the radio show Eileen listens to (100-101).  Examine the psychologist's and listeners' comments for evidence of illogical reasoning.  Consider especially the following cases:

    (a)  The caller who wonders if she should demand that her boyfriend pay more attention to her.

    (b)  The caller who wants to know whether to trust her father.

    (c)  The caller whose girlfriend is pregnant.

    (d)  The caller who says she must work.

    (e)  The caller who sees nothing wrong with a single mother having children.

(f) The caller who insists that her boyfriend buy her a diamond ring.

7. Sometimes in the study of critical thinking, students begin to suspect that a good thinker approaches every issue with cold, hard logic. The focus of Chapter 3 is on the role of emotions in the thinking process. Often we think of our feelings as one thing and our intellect as another. Watkins seems to believe that those aspects are interrelated. In fact, he suggests that an empathetic person will make more objective decisions. He implies that a critical thinker with a "good heart" tends to see issues from several perspectives and considers the bigger picture. The radio psychologist, on the other hand, appears to believe that reason and emotion are separate and should remain so. She suggests that emotions can often interfere with careful decision making. What do you think? Is one wrong and the other right? Are they both right? Is neither? What role do emotions play in our thinking process?

8. One of the key issues in Chapter 3 is context, the circumstances in which an event occurs. Often those surrounding circumstances give an event its meaning. For example, the sound of a pencil point scratching on a sheet of paper may mean nothing to you. But if that sound is coming from the student next to you in a math test that has you completely baffled, you might find that sound very irritating. It may, in fact, serve to further stifle your ability to answer the questions. The context of language can also alter its meaning. The word "girl," for example might or might not be offensive depending on who uses it, to whom, in what situation, and where. Some words might be censored in certain contexts. Can you think of any? Watkins suggest that almost all judgments must take into account the context. Do you agree? Do you believe that there are moral absolutes that are independent of context? Can you give some examples? Do you believe, instead, that context should govern our judgments? Can you defend that claim? Is there a difference between Watkins's use of "context" in grading Gary Kardell's essay (Chapter 2) and the "context" that we use to judge someone's language or behavior?

### The Writing Process

1. After the mock-confrontation in which Watkins calls the students names, he states: "Now you know what it fees like to be called names. Could you have gotten that feeling if I'd come in and said 'It doesn't feel good to be harassed verbally?" (90) Can the same statement be made about the kind of writing which "shows" the reader rather than "tells"?

2. Referring to question 1, what are some other techniques you might employ to make the reader "feel" pain, fear, empathy, or, indeed, a number of other emotions?

3. Evaluating Eileen's paper (100), Watkins cites both the strengths and the weaknesses of her effort. Explore his reasoning. Do you believe this is a fair, insightful assessment.

4. If John were to have written about his fears instead of waiting for the point when "the dam burst" (103), do you think he may have found in his writing a "therapeutic" affect similar to Eileen's in her papers?

5. Although Nick has just implored John to "get involved," and stop being a spectator, as he is sitting in class, John is aware that he is missing "a chance to comment on his own notion that you didn't have to experience everything if you had an imagination" (104). Do you see that perhaps this notion keeps him from "getting involved" in his writing? The novel seems to suggest that we can use our imaginations for opposite reasons: first, to empathize with others and to imagine what it must be like to be someone else; and second, to escape the world of pain or heartache or loss, to enter a fantasy world. John seems to use his imagination as escape. Is it a view that uses imagination to "evade" rather than to look within honestly? Will writing for John be evasive rather than therapeutic?

### Topics for Writing

1. Defending his mock verbal assault, Watkins claims that this method was necessary to let students "know what it feels like to

191

be called names." Write a paper in which you clearly describe a situation in which you were made uncomfortable or were hurt emotionally. Try to show how you felt and evoke sympathy or empathy in the reader.

2. "But sometimes," Watkins asserts, "in judging the behaviors or the reaction of others, it helps to have walked in their shoes, or at least imagined what it must be like to be that person" (91). With this statement in mind, choose a person to write about. Perhaps, you initially judged a person incorrectly because you did not imagine what it must be like to be that person."

3. "Should we judge your comments," Jessica asks, "on what you meant or how we felt" (89). Write about an incident in which you "intended" one thing but were misinterpreted, or an incident in which you misinterpreted at first what was intended by the other person or persons.

4. Despite the radio psychologist's contention that we should always control our emotions (101), this is not always possible (nor, certainly, always desirable). Eileen argues that we have to forgive a momentary lapse in sensitivity, which sometimes is caused by not controlling emotions. Write about an incident in which you lost control of your emotions. What was the consequence? Did you learn a lesson

5. "I'm afraid of everything," John blurts out to Nick in a pivotal passage (103). Indicate your fears; what do they say about you as a person? Have you taken any steps to control these fears?

6. Recalling Nick's admonition to John: "You can't always be a spectator" (103), explore a situation in which you took a stand against some injustice. Explain the incident, why you rebelled, and how you felt at each stage.

7. One way to "get involved" is to use your writing to speak out against injustice. Write a paper that protests against some situation. Perhaps, imagine that you will be sending your paper to a college or local newspaper. Employ concrete examples to show the reader what is wrong; indicate what steps you propose to bring about improvement or correction.

## Questions for Discussion

1. "Thrilled" to discover his students still talking about the racial incident, Watkins is at first "disappointed" but then not surprised at the natural ebb and flow of interest that young people—no, all people—show towards serious events" (85). Consider the following questions: 1) do we tend to forget serious issues too quickly, and if so, why; and 2) are young people less likely or more likely to forget compared to older people?

2. "If they involve you directly," Jennifer asserts, we are more likely to sustain an interest in serious issues (87). This is echoed in Watkins's comment: "Unless you've been there, you might not know what it's like." Do we avoid serious issues because they do not affect us personally; do we avoid them because we have not "walked in the shoes" of other people? Do we have a shortage of empathy?

3. "If there were a manual for teaching college, this predicament would not be in it. Not only was the class taking this in a direction he had not anticipated; the focus was on him" (89). As uncomfortable as Watkins is feeling, do you think he has "stumbled" onto an instructive class lesson? Does it lead to more of a clarification of the issues?

4. Again, Watkins reveals himself to be less than the all-knowing professor of the TV and film stereotypes in the second paragraph of page 92. Indeed, he also displays rather overtly his discomfort: "He blew out his cheeks and sighed long and loudly, a sight at which several students giggled." Nevertheless, does this discussion seem to be working? How would you evaluate his over-all performance in this discussion?

5. Perhaps you have in your school experience heard teachers claim that sometimes they learn from their students. You may or may not have believed that claim. But is just such an experience portrayed in the discussion that takes place on page 89?

6.  Reacting to John's admission of fear, Nick counsels him to get more involved: "You can't always be just a spectator" (103). Do we tend to be spectators too often? Explore times when you have gotten involved and other times when you were a spectator. Consider some of your feelings at the time and also other people's reactions.

7.  "Well, I think some teachers do go too far in trying to prove a point," Belinda comments (89). Can we expect reasonable limits; do teachers sometimes need to "shake things up"? If they wish to make an important point, should teachers feel free to resort to "dramatics"?

8.  How do you respond to Watkins's comment: "I think the ability to establish guidelines and criteria comes from having a good head on your shoulders, but I think the ability to consider the context comes from having a good heart" (92)?

## Understanding the Novel

1.  While the verbal barrage (87) is clearly out of character for the mild-mannered Watkins, do we still see that this approach is consistent with his goals as a teacher?

2.  Consider the parallels the author draws between Watkins who "suddenly felt comfortable enough or brave enough" to choose a student to answer his question (88) with John's admission of fear in the dam bursting speech (103).

3.  Does Pete Churnip misinterpret Watkins's comment to the class: "Wow, you guys are good. You're very good" (90). What does this exchange suggest about the relationship of teacher and students?

4.  Thanking Eileen for "coming to my defense," Watkins surprises her by showing a side of teachers she never suspected. Do you see this statement as a surprise? In what way does it undercut or contradict the stereotypical notion of teachers? (97)

5. Before leaving campus, Eileen acts on Watkins's suggestion and works with a tutor in the Writing Lab (99). Contrast this with John's unwillingness to accept the professor's advice about showing him more drafts and revisions. Can you account for John's resistance

6. After listening to the radio doctor's comments, Eileen "concentrated hard on remembering the doctor's words. She thought she might tell Watkins what he was missing" (100). What is it that she wants to tell Watkins?

7. Berating John for ignoring Jen's pleas for support in the class discussion, Nick exclaims: "This was your chance to stand up for something" (101). Why does Jen need help? What does this passage suggest about the strength of the friendship between Nick and John?

8. What further information does the author provide us about John in the passage in which John explains that he is fearful of everything (103)? In terms of John's growing process, how important is this confession?

9. Do you see parallels between Watkins's statement: "I think the ability to consider the context comes from having a good heart" (92) with Eileen's personality: her papers, her plea to forgive people?

10. Although she had been so involved in the class discussion earlier, Jen brushes aside John's apology for not supporting her, as she worries about Parents' Weekend. Why, do you surmise, has she not told her parents about Nick?

# CHAPTER IV

*Questions for Critical Thinking*

1. Although Watkins and Eileen resist their impulse to believe that Tony Falcone is responsible for ransacking Jim Washington's room, it's hard not to jump to the conclusion that Tony was somehow involved. When you first read the newspaper account of the incident, did you, too, assume that Tony may have been responsible? What evidence is presented to lead you toward that conclusion? If you did suspect Tony, what does that say about our willingness to consider all possible perspectives?

2. Watkins's discussion with Betty reveals her to be less-than-logical thinker. What fallacy is central to her reasoning? What kind of thinker is she? Consider especially the following points:

    a) She ignores the racial incident to discuss the football game.

    b) She argues that "that kind of thing happens every day."

    c) She says "I would never do it" and argues that African-Americans can be racist, too.

    d) She upbraids Watkins with the reminder that other things need speaking out against.

*The Writing Process*

In the conversation between Watkins and John's mother it is revealed that John has "invented" a personality: we see now the reason for his persistent reluctance to confer with Watkins or accept his constructive criticism. From the first, the teacher's advice to explore an aspect of John's father cannot be followed because he has chosen to escape the reality by constructing an imaginary father and, indeed an imaginary world. Explore how the escapist path has prevented John from "looking within" and being "honest"; how the "gem of an idea" could never be developed because self-discovery was not valued. How has his approach deprived him of any therapeutic affect: had he looked within earlier, might he have discovered the need to take risks and to get involved?

### Topics for Writing

1. Although his mother initially "held his face in both hands and kissed his cheeks and forehead as if he were five years old," notice that the relationship between John and his mother, appears in some other ways as one between two adults—a more equal relationship in which ideas are rather openly and easily discussed (108-109). You might try to catch a moment, a slice of life, which represents an aspect of your relationship with one of your parents. You might also want to look at the discussion that begins on page 125.

2. "Don't generalize and stereotype, John. What would Watkins think?" Eileen says to John (110). Actually, Watkins would be pleased that Eileen is definitely getting something out of her education because she is applying her learning in college to other aspects of her life. Write about one or two recent intellectual discoveries which you have been able to apply directly to your own life.

3. "Well, here's your big moment. It's time to grow up," Nick tells John (130). Can you pinpoint a moment in your life that seemed to usher in adulthood? Describe the situation fully and try to deal with your thoughts and feelings at the time.

4. Nick's advice in the previous question defines an important element in friendship: being responsible and caring enough to take the risk of telling a friend something he or she might not want to hear. Have you either given a friend important advice of this nature or received such advice? What were the consequences?

5. Accepting Mike's invitation to play golf, Peter Watkins appears to enlist one more activity to feed his habit of procrastination, but he also seems to "play the part"—live up to other people's expecta-

tions or do something which pleases another person. Perhaps he also feels it is something he should be able to do. Write about such a situation in your experience. Watkins suffered embarrassment; what were some of the emotions you experienced?

6. "What am I going to do? he thought" (128). Though it entails taking risks and overcoming fears, at a pivotal moment in the novel, John must decide whether he can do the right thing. Consider such a moment in your own life, or explore what would be some of the deciding factors or "bottom lines" for you to take action.

### Questions for Discussion

1. Having admired her from a safe distance, John finally hears the first words Eileen speaks to him: "John, isn't it? I think you're in my writing class" (111). In this question and through question 6, refer to this introduction, John's awkwardness, and the conversation about John's "sexy" mother. First, what steps do you take, successfully or not, to control your own nervousness or shyness in attempting to establish rapport with the opposite gender?

2. Is John accurate or is he a victim of gender stereotyping in his response to Eileen's observation that his mother is sexy: "Well, women can say those things and get away with it." In this scene has Eileen already escaped gender-based roles?

3. Do you see parallels between the sports spectacles of John in tennis and Watkins in golf? Are they the consequence of both adhering to what is expected of males in our society? Can you think of activities you are locked into because of gender-based expectations?

4. Do we too often conform to the role playing that society expects of men and women? Does this prevent us from communicating with each other, first, as individuals and, second, as males and females? Should we be more gender-blind? Do you see a parallel between gender "blindness" and "color" or "race" blindness?

5. In what ways, if any, are you willing to depart from the "script" in terms of gender role playing? What is the response of others to such choices that you make?

6. "Don't generalize and stereotype, John. What would Watkins think?" Eileen comments. This comment may strike some readers as odd, since we don't always make connections between what we study in class and what happens to us in our daily lives. Does it appear sometimes that what you are studying is "divorced" from real life? Can you cite examples both to confirm and to contradict this question?

7. Responding to John's description of overhearing the details of the room ransacking, his mother asks: "What are you going to do?" Does it strike you that this question—in fact questioning itself— differs from some parental responses? Do parents tend to rush in and tell children what to do or at least to offer advice perhaps too quickly? How would you characterize the parent-child relationship revealed in this passage?

8. Referring back to question 7, address the legitimate question "What are you going to do?" In other words, given a similar situation, would you take action, risk consequences, speak out? What would be the basis of your actions? Have you encountered situations in which you now feel you should have "said something"? Have you witnessed events in which you considered intervening, but did nothing? Why? What made you incapable of acting?

9. Do you see a parallel between the parent-child relationship discussed above and the type of relationship Watkins establishes with his students? Is this a desirable relationship; does it contribute to the learning process?

### Understanding the Novel

1. John may have solid reason to think he has botched his first conversation with Eileen (111). Some might suggest that he personifies in this scene an inept, awkward "geek," but in the course of this chapter, how does Eileen actually process John's behavior?

2. At this point in the novel what, would you surmise, are Watkins's feelings about Diane (112). In what way does he seem to be failing to take his own advice to John to take risks?

3. What does the conversation between Watkins and John's mother reveal about John? Does it explain his resistance to Watkins's writing methods and to Nick's insistence on his getting involved?

4. "Well, actually she should listen to you," replies Eileen to Watkins, who misunderstands the compliment (117). What does she mean by this remark: in what way is the radio psychologist wrong and Watkins right?

5. Paralleling John's humiliation at tennis, Watkins undertakes a humorous golf-teeing activity. What comparisons can you make between these two spectacular failures?

6. What further parallels do you see between John and Watkins in the first paragraph of page 124: "Watkins was overcome with the desire to communicate with someone, but he didn't know anyone at work well enough to phone." Again does he fail to take his own advice—"to get involved"?

7. "Well, here's your big moment. It's time to grow up," Nick warns John (130). What do your surmise are some of John's thought processes as he makes his decision, which is not revealed until the next chapter, five weeks later. What are some of the issues he needs to sort out?

# CHAPTER V

*Questions for Critical Thinking*

1. From the beginning of *Parallel Lives*, characters have judged and responded to other characters based on assumptions. At the very start of the novel, John draws conclusions about Watkins and Eileen based on his observations and his assumptions. Now, at the end of the novel, your own assumptions as a reader are tested. Were you shocked to discover something about Nick's identity that had not been revealed earlier? Or did you have some notion of what was coming? The book is filled with clues, but you may have missed them. Now that you know the ending, can you recall any evidence that you overlooked?

2. Does the fact that you may be surprised at Nick's identity reveal anything else about you as a reader or thinker? Are you incredulous at the discovery of Nick's identity because you would have expected him to act and speak and think in a different way? Do your expectations conform to a stereotype?

3. The tendency to generalize and to group people into manageable categories is probably our most common—and our weakest—trait as thinkers. Very few of us are free from the habit of mind that causes us to try to make sense of a chaotic and disorganized world by classifying and categorizing what we see, including people. We sometimes speak in broad terms about "them," or "us," or "you." In defending her generation, how does Jessica avoid generalizing? How does Watkins avoid generalizing as he watches his students leave the classroom for the last time?

4. One of the novel's themes is that knowledge—and critical reasoning skills—are useless without action. The smartest, most rational man or woman does the world little good if he or she does nothing, writes nothing, teaches nothing. John, at the start of the novel, avoids contact with others; by the end he appears on the verge of a life of action and participation. In what ways can you use your critical thinking skills to more actively participate in your world? What activities can a critical thinker undertake to make a difference in his or her life and the lives of others?

5.  A few significant scenes in the final chapter involve the evaluation of both students and teachers. From what you've seen of Watkins's evaluation of student writing (Eileen's essays, Gary Kardell's, John's), what do you think he believes makes an effective piece of written communication? Are all of his criteria objective, or does he also grade according to his subjective responses? If so, can you describe them? Do you think he is a fair grader? Watkins himself is evaluated during the last class by his students. The novel does not include the criteria for evaluating a teacher, but you can probably create one based on what you've read and what you've experienced in your own life. What makes a good teacher?

6.  Why is evaluating the performance of others such a difficult task? What's the difference between judging and being judgmental?

7.  From a critical thinking standpoint, did you learn anything from reading *Parallel Lives*? Would you call it a good book?

### *The Writing Process*

1.  Having worried endlessly about his grades, though he doesn't yet know it, John receives an A+ on his final paper (156). Referring back to the Writing Process sections of Chapter 4, consider these two questions as you look closely at the paragraph from John's paper: first, does this passage confirm your earlier response? and, second, how does John's paragraph reveal his acknowledgement of the various elements of good writing emphasized repeatedly by Watkins?

2.  In what important respect do we see a correlation again between learning and life in this passage: what connection can you make, for instance, between "taking risks" expressed in John's paper and significant risks that he takes as we learn from Chapter 5?

3.  Agonizing over his attempt to call Eileen for a date, John momentarily considers a disguise. Nick tells him: "Be yourself, you lunatic" (137). Later, John says to Watkins, "Well, remember how you told me that I shouldn't make up stories in essays?" (143). As in the previous question concerning learning and life, consider

what steps John takes to give up escapism and dare to "be him-self."

## Topics for Writing

1. Recalling his chest of turkey gaffe, John thinks "there was reason to laugh, and he knew it. He had started to laugh with them, and the memory now caused him to chuckle" (137). We have dis-cussed the understandable desire to "fit in," but do you possess some personality traits that you accept as inevitable—that you can live with and even laugh at?

2. It is suggested in the final class discussion that your generation is more accepting of diversity. Does the friendship between John and Nick substantiate Jessica's contention: "I'm talking about a one-on-one level. Individuals can overcome their prejudices. You have to start somewhere, and maybe our generation is the place to start" (150)?

3. Confiding in his younger colleague, Professor Golden despairs about "the apparent disdain with which his students considered their education and perhaps their educators" (141). Watkins re-plies: "I don't know, Walt. Have you asked them?" Would it be a good idea to ask them? What might their (and your) answer be?

4. As he shocks himself and virtually everyone else, John rescues Watkins with his remark: "He's generalizing. . . . Maybe he's con-centrating too much on the negative, and not enough on what's really great about this generation" (148). Although we hear la-menting by parents, educators, psychologists—especially radio psychologists—is John correct that there are considerable posi-tives about your generation. You might also want to refer to Wat-kins's thoughts on pages 152-153.

5. From your perspective about college at this stage, can you imag-ine ever echoing John's comment: "A lot has happened to me this semester. I think I grew up more in two months than I did in the eighteen years before that. (142). For John the experience has been heightened through remarkable events, but as you continue your college experience, do you think you might be more willing

to agree with Watkins's assertion "that there is more to college than just grades"?

6. "Would they learn to dance every day to the extraordinary music of their lives?" wonders Watkins in his reflection about the fates of his students. Does John's passage about the writing process also suggest his attitude about life and in a way respond to Watkins's musing? Write your own response to Watkins's question.


## Questions for Discussion

Now that you have completed the novel, you are encouraged, particularly from your unique perspective as students, to share certain critical observations in response to the following questions.

1. Do you see the author's portrayal of college students as accurate and realistic? To be sure, the author contradicts the unflattering stereotype of such films as *Animal House*, but, nevertheless, does he "get it right"?

2. Similarly, many literary and film portrayals of teachers tend to present them in an "idyllic" fashion as in the famous work, *Goodbye, Mr. Chipps*. While Watkins is in many ways "ideal," do you think he is more "human" and even more flawed than the stereotypical representation of teachers? Is Watkins a composite of different teachers, or is he a realistic portrayal of some teachers?

3. Do you support the notion of college presented in the book-that it is much more than an academic experience, or is this too idealistic a notion, one that teachers might believe, but not students?

4. Wending your way through this book, you have been exposed to a particular writing process espoused by Professor Watkins. Has this been helpful to your own progress in writing? What elements, if any, do you reject? What elements in particular have been beneficial?

5. As in the previous question, consider the possible advantages that you may have derived in having such a text. Did you find, perhaps, that the third chapter serves almost as a critical thinking

laboratory: students were asked to apply their learning about good thinking processes directly to the incident at hand? Is such a practical approach to critical thinking helpful?

### Understanding the Novel

The questions in this section are intended mainly as a wrap-up for the entire novel though some demand attention to the critical events that occur in the final chapter.

1. Surprise endings have always been a favorite device of novelists. How do you respond to the last scene: do you share the surprise or even shock of John's mother? Or is your reaction more similar to John's: "Huh? Oh, I guess it just never came up" (161).

2. Authors often trace important "evolutions" or development of their characters from the beginning of a novel to the end in respect to the attainment of new insights, maturity, and potential. Such character development is particularly evident in the portrayals of Peter Watkins, John, and Eileen. What new realizations do these characters come to in the final chapter and what new steps do they take that give evidence of significant growth? Consider Watkins's letter to Diane; John's reporting the ransacking incident, changing his major and working up the courage to ask Eileen for a date; and Eileen's saying good-bye to the radio doctor and encouraging her grandmother to communicate.

3. Again, now that you have completed the novel, what would you say are the most striking parallels between John and Watkins? Is the title of the book most appropriate in terms of this set of parallels? What significance do you ascribe to the author's drawing of parallels?

4. Referring to the previous question, what do you think are some of the most important parallels the author draws between Watkins and Eileen?

5. Another authorial device is to portray significant contrasts between the main character and another character. What importance do you see in the contrast between John and Nick?

6. Everyone, universally and from century to century "likes a story." Did you find the story interesting? Did you want to know what was coming next? Were you involved with the characters, hoping that things would turn out well for them?

7. Sometimes humor makes a novel more pleasing. What are some of your favorite examples of humor in the book: while they are funny, do these instances also serve to underscore plot, character, or theme?

8. Sometimes—but this is very, very rare—authors don't say a thing! Note the following conversation, starting with Watkins's comment: "my pleasure, John.' John opened the door. 'Oh, John?'
'Yes.'
'Uh... nothing. Thanks. I'll see you Thursday." (145)
Is this dialogue perhaps more effective than actually spelling out what might be said? What is it that might be said?

9. Authors often like to work with symbols. Comment on the effectiveness of the following: "As John talked, Watkins watched him twist and fidget in the chair, place one leg across the other, shake his foot and tug at his cap. Finally, John placed his palm on top of the cap and pushed it back on his head so that the bill was completely off his face" (142).